More than a Mama

Chhavi Mittal is a renowned film and television actor who has ventured into the world of content creation with her YouTube channel, Shitty Ideas Trending, which she runs with her husband Mohit Hussein. After successfully adapting the sitcom format to YouTube, she went on to become one of the foremost content creators on Facebook in India. Mittal created waves again on social media during her second pregnancy with her remarkable post-partum recovery and fitness regime. She is known to have a warm heart and a good head on her shoulders. She is also known to fight for social causes and is considered a good public speaker as well. After becoming a mother of two, she took it upon herself to help address issues related to motherhood and launched a company, Being Woman, to promote true fitness and a positive body image. Mittal was diagnosed with breast cancer in 2022 and was lauded for the way she fought the disease while sharing her recovery journey on social media. Today, Mittal stands tall as a self-made entrepreneur, inspiring personality and a certified Steiner educator. This book is an effort to share her motherhood, post-partum and fitness journey with the world.

A Memoir of Motherhood

CHHAVI MITTAL

Published by
Rupa Publications India Pvt. Ltd 2023
7/16, Ansari Road, Daryaganj
New Delhi 110002

Sales centres:
Bengaluru Chennai
Hyderabad Jaipur Kathmandu
Kolkata Mumbai Prayagraj

Copyright © Chhavi Mittal 2023

While every effort has been made to verify the authenticity of the information contained in this book, it is not intended as a substitute for medical consultation with a physician. The publisher and the author are in no way liable for the use of the information contained in this book.

The views and opinions expressed in this book are the author's own and the facts are as reported by her which have been verified to the extent possible, and the publishers are not in any way liable for the same.

All rights reserved.
No part of this publication may be reproduced, transmitted, or stored in a retrieval system, in any form or by any means, electronic, mechanical, photocopying, recording or otherwise, without the prior permission of the publisher.

P-ISBN: 978-93-5702-528-7
E-ISBN: 978-93-5702-527-0

First impression 2023

10 9 8 7 6 5 4 3 2 1

The moral right of the author has been asserted.

Printed in India

This book is sold subject to the condition that it shall not, by way of trade or otherwise, be lent, resold, hired out, or otherwise circulated, without the publisher's prior consent, in any form of binding or cover other than that in which it is published.

*Dedicated to my mother, Veena Mittal,
who has taught me everything*

Contents

Introduction		ix
1.	Being a Mother: When is the Right Time?	1
2.	Being Pregnant: The Facts and Myths	19
3.	Developing the Mind–Body Connection	41
4.	The Importance of Diet during Pregnancy	64
5.	Post-partum Fitness: Slow and Steady Wins the Race	87
6.	Being Healthy: Post-partum Diet	111
7.	Post-partum Depression and Mental Wellness	134
8.	The Art of Time Management	157
Acknowledgements		169

Introduction

I was fortunate enough to be reborn without physically leaving this world. In fact, there are many women like me. If you are reading this book, chances are that you've been as lucky too, or perhaps you are on your way to being as lucky in the near future. No prizes for guessing that I am talking about being a mother. Motherhood gives you another opportunity to relive your life, undoing the mistakes you have made in the past, relearning everything from scratch, only this time from a different, more mature perspective.

I am a mother of two adorable kids, and I feel truly blessed that they chose me to be their mother. As each day passes, thanks to them, I get to add a new feather to my cap.

Where do I even begin my story? The surge of energy I feel every morning is something I never knew I had in me. I can achieve things I found daunting earlier despite the multiple roles that I play in my daily life—from running the house to running two companies; from taking care of two absolutely wonderful children to finding a balance in my own life.

We should use the word 'daunting' to describe what many women feel at the prospect of becoming a mother. There is so much information floating around about motherhood that some of it can make a perfectly capable woman change her mind. I know women who worry too much about how things are going to be once they become mothers. Time management, juggling between career and personal growth, losing the personal life they have had so far or the fear of losing their slender bodies forever—these are only a few of the worries that women have. And then there are also some who do not think about the future at all and just take the plunge.

Well, for all those who are reading this, I have good news. I am a living example of somebody who not only successfully overcame all her doubts but also accomplished a lot more than I had ever envisioned! In this book, I

Introduction

take you through my journey and talk about my own struggles and doubts. But more importantly, I describe how motherhood empowered me to take control of my life and turn my issues around in my favour, while also realizing the importance of things that are actually meaningful. Among other things, I share my diet, my exercise routine, my emotional struggles, the post-partum depression I experienced, the 'dos and don'ts' I learnt while being pregnant and the several myths that I successfully busted during my pregnancy. Over the course of this book, you will become acquainted not only with me but also my darling husband, Mohit Hussein, who is a pillar of strength for me and my little ones, Areeza and Arham.

While I am not a certified nutritionist or a therapist or a doctor, I surely am one of you who walked her own path and discovered something new and wonderful. My findings are purely based on my own experiences, my research and the books I have read. My endeavour through this book is to make you capable of creating your own unique path. I hope you will be able to create your own diet and a workout plan and chalk out a routine that is best suited and customized for your own needs. As

I elaborate on my journey in the chapters that follow, remember to listen to your own body every step of the way. Read on, dear women.

I

Being a Mother: When is the Right Time?

Being a mother is the greatest feeling in the world. However, before a woman becomes a mother, she must consider many things. Is she ready to take on the responsibility of another life? Is she physically fit to do that? Is she mentally prepared for the toughest job in the world? As baffling as these questions sound, I was undaunted by them. It was not because I was extremely brave, it was simply because I had no idea that these things needed to be considered!

To me, the choices were pretty simple:

1. Do we want a baby?
2. Or do we not?

As newlyweds, my husband Mohit and I chose the second option. We decided that we were really happy with what we had and did not want to pressurize ourselves or change anything about the way we lived. After all, who wants to let go of the more important things in life like being free, living for oneself, having the luxury of wanting to wake up in Goa one day and be able to drive down at 2.00 a.m.? We did not want to lose simple pleasures like playing loud music in the house and hosting parties that could last till beyond sunrise, where we could invite friends over for dinner and serve breakfast as well!

Yet, seven years later, still in love with each other and the crazy lifestyle that we had, we toyed with the two options once again. I remember it was because I met a friend for lunch who told me that there is nothing more fulfilling than having a child. He painted a picture that looked so rosy and enticing. 'Chhavi,' he said, 'no matter what you achieve in life, the happiness that a child hugging you brings to you when you reach home after a tough day

Being a Mother: When is the Right Time?

is nothing compared to all the riches of the world.' That was it. I kept thinking about those words and imagining myself as a mother. I could hardly imagine being able to start a new chapter in my life; albeit an exciting one that could bring me so much fulfilment. For days, I kept picturing myself as a mom. I saw myself holding a little baby in my arms, sitting on a park bench, my hair flying gently in the breeze, and Mohit standing a little away, clicking a picture that captured the beautiful, dreamy moment. One fine day, I mustered up the courage to tell Mohit that I wanted to be a mother if he would like to be a father. I will never forget the words that came out of his mouth. 'I've been waiting for you to say this for over a year now.' And just like that, this time, we chose the first option. On our seventh anniversary, we found out that we were pregnant with our first baby!

Suddenly, the life that I had been living for the past few years felt like a waste. I couldn't remember why we took so long to take this decision. It couldn't have been the parties or the erratic working hours because we still had those. It couldn't have been the urge to go for mini vacations because we continued those as well. The reason we took so long to take the decision to start a family, I realized, was that we were simply not ready then. Choosing the right time to start my journey as a mother was one of the biggest reasons why my pregnancy was such a happy one.

In my opinion, the only reason to have a baby should be that you feel ready as a couple. It should not be just because it is the obvious next step or because it is the right thing to do. It should not be because 'Payal and Sameer had a baby and so should we!' It is not a race to see who comes first and who gets left behind. It should not be because the biological clock is ticking. It should definitely not be a reaction to the pressure put on couples by relatives saying, '*Khush khabri kab suna rahe ho* (When are you giving us the good news)?' or obligations towards ailing parents, blackmailing you emotionally saying, '*Marne se pehle pote ka munh dikha de* (Let me see my grandchild's face before I die)!' Such statements by relatives are nothing more than typical conversation topics for most of them, something as banal as a 'How are you?' or 'How's life?'. The 'ailing' parents, in all probability, are perfectly hale and hearty, but they say such things because other people, especially in old Hindi movies, say so. Let's face it, such statements are

Being a Mother: When is the Right Time?

pretty darn melodramatic and how can anyone pass up the opportunity to say all of that? In fact, when we got pregnant the first time, my father-in-law shed happy tears when we broke the news. He confided in us that he had started to believe that we had medical issues and had gone to the extent of asking for a *mannat* for divine intervention, even though he is quite an agnostic! Such was his desire to become a grandfather. Thank goodness we did not succumb to any of those pressures, because raising a child should solely be the decision of the couple that is going to commit to being parents for the rest of their lives. Succumbing to those pressures would have meant having a child at the wrong time.

Although you feel physically and mentally ready, there may be other reasons that hinder you from going down this road. One of the biggest reasons is job unpredictability or financial instability. Often, we tend to plan for the future and forget to live in the present. I was no different. In a lot of ways, I am still that way. I find myself deriving more happiness from the perfectly created schedule for the upcoming week than the perfectly executed present day. Many believe that it is only fair to have a solid plan in place for unborn children before you even start thinking about having them. Such a plan could be different for different people. It could comprise a comfortable house, with a yard for the child to play in, a decent school in the vicinity, a car to drive the child to school and back or, at the very least, a school bus service that operates between home and the school.

A stable source of income to pay the high fees that schools demand these days is also important for many. One also has to take into consideration the increasing cost of baby essentials—cots, playpens, perambulators, walkers, toys, tricycles, bicycles, etc.—and the fact that babies grow up surprisingly fast!

Another reason, which should actually be the topmost but is very often forgotten, is the time at hand. Having a baby means you need to have time. Time to take the child to the park, time to teach him or her how to walk and how to sleep, sit, stand, run, eat, drink from a bottle, drink from a cup, talk, brush his teeth, cycle, swim, play football, basketball, badminton, table tennis or whatever else you fancy. Dancing, painting or singing can be left to extracurricular classes that you can enrol the child in, but that too requires money. Time and money are also needed for vacations because, unfortunately, schools have

Being a Mother: When is the Right Time?

summer holidays (which offices don't) and these holidays make children impatient. Then there's also the competition among kids as to who went to the best destination during their vacations and who got the best vacation gifts.

Well, to be honest, I realized all of these things only *after* I had the baby. I still remember going for the first birthday party with my daughter. (Oh yes, there's a plethora of these and they require you to maintain a completely different kind of decorum, which I'm still learning. I am positive that I will master this someday.) At the party, I spoke with fellow first-time mothers of six-month-olds, discussing school admissions for their kids. This was a completely different world for me! I had a knot in my stomach when I realized that I was too late to get my child admitted to a good school because, apparently, these forms should have been filled when I had been pregnant! What had I been doing then?

I had been busy enjoying my dreamy pregnancy, which, now I realize, is something that all those mothers had forgotten to do because they had been busy making plans—plans for the future, financial plans, education plans, buying-a-house plans, shifting-to-a-better job plans, plans for playschools, primary schools, higher education, marriage, grandchildren, the list goes on. And even though they spent so much time planning, they still had kids quite early in their marriage. I could only imagine how soon into their marriage they must have started to plan.

As lost as I felt at that time, here's what I think. In my opinion, the right time for family planning does not depend on future planning as much as it depends on being mentally and physically ready. As the popular quote by Allen Saunders goes: 'Life is what happens to us while we are busy making other plans.' Although I had always been a planner, after becoming a mother, I started making only those plans that helped me live in the moment. While I realized that I had missed doing so many bigger things that other well-equipped parents had done, like school admission, investments, having a bigger and nicer house, and many smaller things, like setting up a nursery in preparation for the little one's arrival, I also realized that I was thoroughly enjoying each and every moment of Areeza growing up. I wasn't bothered about what was the right age for her to teethe, or to start walking, talking, self-feeding, let alone things like what is the right age to go to school, which school, which school board, etc. I grew up as Areeza grew up. I

Being a Mother: When is the Right Time?

learnt everything at her pace. I did everything at the right time. No wonder then that I enjoyed my first pregnancy like a queen.

Before I got pregnant, I had signed a TV show as the leading lady on the number one network in the country at the time. I did not plan for it but found myself opting out because I had that choice. Instead, I started going for long, relaxing walks, many of which were in the comfort of malls. I joined a yoga class for pregnant mothers. I joined a prenatal Lamaze class. I was pampered by everyone I knew, and I knew a lot of people (all those parties that I had hosted into the wee hours of the morning had not been for naught). It was a pregnancy that one can only dream of. There were no complications, I looked lovely, I felt amazing and I was on my way to becoming a mother! As a bonus, my hair grew at the speed at which Rapunzel's must have grown. What more could I ask for? I had absolutely no complaints whatsoever. After all, this was the first time in seven years that I had free time. And I was still not planning for the future. The mere fact that I wasn't aware of any of the responsibilities that lay ahead made me practically float at all times, feeling like a blessed angel. From somebody who was used to working

40 days a month to somebody who did not know what to do with her time, it was a huge change, though a welcome one.

The pregnancy was like lying down on a beautiful float in a giant pool and sunbathing. However, when the baby was born, it was almost like being pushed into the deep end. I realized why some of the best swimmers learnt swimming when they were pushed into the deep end. I quickly equipped myself with all the things I needed to be a hands-on mother. Once I had Areeza, I found myself slowly but surely considering each of the things that I would hear mothers talk about at birthday parties. I learnt one stroke at a time while also enjoying the swim. I did not plan how I would learn the next stroke until I mastered the one at hand. I did not pressure myself at any point. I gave myself time and allowed myself to fail because failure is the first step to success. When the right time came, I found myself investing towards a better future while also house hunting. I found myself setting a routine for little Areeza and teaching her all the things that I felt she was ready to learn at each stage. When the right time came, I found the school best suited for her needs and my convenience, and I also found myself buying that family car.

Being a Mother: When is the Right Time?

My most important learning from all these things was how to live my life in the present, not the future. I found myself becoming a sensible, mature person, who stopped being frivolous and started realizing the importance of other aspects of life. By other aspects, I do not mean finances or material things, but things like peace and contentment. I learnt that when you become a parent, you include a third person in your life, who is, henceforth, going to be a part of your life—a part of each of your smiles and sorrows. This person should be happy no matter what kind of house you live in, what mode of transportation you use, what school she goes to or what her family outings look like, as long as they are with both her parents and maybe her grandparents. This child is going to grow up one day at a time and will learn skills that will help her survive in the real world. This child will move houses with you, and even move cities or countries with you if your job or heart demands it. How then can planning things like finances and jobs become crucial in making that decision to start a family?

While I understand that every parent wants to give the best to their child, I also understand that as a mother, my job is just to gently guide my child into being able to take care of herself. And I could only do this if I decided to have a baby on my own terms, as per my time, when I felt ready, both physically as well as mentally. No amount of future planning could have saved me had I decided to get pregnant even a year before I was ready. I still sometimes think about the things that could have gone wrong in my life had I got pregnant earlier. I had the extra space and money (because I did have those things) and I was a certain number of years into my marriage. Frustration? Unhappiness? Pressures for which I may not have been ready? What if I found myself succumbing to the pressure of having a second child because the first one was lonely?

This brings me to my next point. When exactly is the right time to have a second child? If you still haven't figured out the answer to this question, you might want to go back and read this entire chapter from the beginning. The reasons are exactly the same. While I completely agree that a sibling is important for a child, that does not mean that having a second child is mandatory! As humans, we learn how to survive and thrive in any situation. Children are the most adaptable. A child will learn to be the only child as beautifully as

Being a Mother: When is the Right Time?

he or she will adapt to being a sibling. I hear parents say that because they grew up with siblings and now have a unique support system, they would like to do the same for their kid as well. I also see many siblings grow up not seeing eye to eye for a multitude of reasons, causing immense mental and emotional stress to each other and the people around them. I even see exemplary siblings who can make an only child forever envious that they do not have a sibling. What I believe is, how you turn out to be, how you shape your life, how you grow up to be, or how lonely, gregarious, sanguine, cheerful, morose or melancholy you are depends on various factors, and having a sibling or not while growing up is just a small part of it. I grew up with two elder siblings but was a lonely child because of the huge age difference between me and them and because of them being closer in age to each other. Have you ever seen a little child crying and throwing a fit to go to a birthday party with their older sibling and the latter getting all annoyed because they cannot have 'mom's spy' accompany them to the party? Well, that little sibling was always me! At the same time, have you experienced being so protected by your older sibling that you were never scared of being bullied or getting into a fight because you knew that the older one will come and get you out before you even bat an eyelid? Well, that too was me. So, basically, having a second child or not is obviously not dependent on the first child. It purely depends on if and when you are ready as a parent. The decision to have a second child is so well defined for some parents that they save the first child's things—like the cot, walker, potty seat, changing table, etc.—in preparation for the next one's arrival. Having a second child was so out of the question for me that I had given away every single belonging of Areeza's that she didn't need. I did not plan for the future and lived in the present. I did have to buy everything all over again when I decided to have Arham, though, which I by no means regret, even though it got me a lot of flak from my husband. The day I shared my thoughts of having a second child with him, Mohit's first reaction was, 'Why did we sell the cot for four thousand bucks then?'

It is important for both parents to be absolutely, one hundred per cent ready to have a second child. The conversations that I had with Mohit about whether or not to extend the family made me realize his fears as a father. His biggest worry was that he would never be able to

Being a Mother: When is the Right Time?

love another human being as much as he loved Areeza. He felt he did not want to be unfair to a little child. This is a very real and practical fear that a parent may have, but in my opinion, it is also something that is not real to a large extent. The decision to have a second baby is only the beginning. The real journey begins when you get pregnant. Watching me pregnant, carrying the baby, watching Areeza bonding with the baby in my belly and taking care of us made Mohit a part of the pregnancy journey. Without a doubt, Mohit's emotions came to the fore the second he held our son in his arms.

My second pregnancy was very different from my first. If I lived through the first one like a queen, I lived through the second one like an empress. By then, I was running a company. While I had the choice to take a back seat, I found myself taking the driver's seat instead. In fact, I started a second company and two new YouTube channels. I devoted all my time and energies to my work and my firstborn. I knew from experience that the best can be experienced only by living for today and not planning for tomorrow. So, I continued to look after the baby in my womb, the child outside of it, and my own health and fitness; I did not worry about how time and other things would be managed once the little one arrived. I did realize, though, that now was the time to kick things up a notch. I started discovering and honing the skills that had been dormant within me. I surprised myself with my organizational skills. I became Chhavi Mittal Version 2.0. Once again, I was reminded of the importance of having a baby at the right time and for the right reasons.

Many mothers ask me if the age gap of six years between my two kids is ideal, and if having a lesser gap would have been better. I can't comment on what works for other couples, but I do know that this age gap is perfect for my family. Besides, an age gap is just a number. No relationship between two siblings has ever depended on this. With a different number, it may work differently, but whether it is good or bad is really dependant on other factors, like upbringing, the mother's state of mind, family atmosphere, diet, challenges, camaraderie between the siblings, etc. Hence, what is important is figuring out the number that is best for you and your situation, and not deciding based on somebody else's experience. And if, for whatever reason, you change your mind and decide against having a second child, you can be happy

Being a Mother: When is the Right Time?

with your decision even if you saved the cot and the pram for four years!

Will I think of having a third child? Well, only time can tell. Once again, I am not going to plan so far ahead for something that may or may not be a possibility. For now, when I bring it up with Mohit, he looks at me as though he wants his money back! 'It's very good that you want to have another baby. Why don't you first find another husband?' he says if I even joke about it! Having a baby is in no way the right decision if both parents are not on the same page, and hence, right now is not the right time for us. If and when we do decide to extend the family further, we will consider the same factors that we considered when I had both my children.

My two pregnancies changed me and my outlook in a big way. It was after I became a mother that I shifted gears from being an actor, who was stuck doing roles that other people thought I could do justice to, to becoming an entrepreneur, creating a roadmap for many others to follow. I discovered my own voice; I had clear ideas and concepts; I even had the courage to say no to things I didn't want to do. I found that by managing my time well, I could devote time to myself, my family, my work, new projects, recreation, socializing, eating and, most importantly, fitness—all with equal elan. I will discuss fitness in depth in the later chapters. But, for now, let's rewind a little to my first pregnancy and tackle some of the common myths I encountered.

2

Being Pregnant: The Facts and Myths

Mohit and I had had a massive fight on the day of our seventh anniversary before he left for his shoot. This was the third day in a row that I had been taking home pregnancy tests, only to be disappointed. However, this time, I was glad I was not pregnant, since I did not know where this particular fight would take us. Like in any relationship, we have our fair share of fights where we exchange filmy dialogues, ending with mature, positive goodbyes stating, 'We'll always be friends', 'we had a good run', etc., that we often look back at and laugh our hearts out. I am not sure if this happens to you, but these are the type of fights where you are convinced that this is the end and that life has come a full circle. You truly believe that you will be one of those really strong women who spend the rest of their lives alone and never need anybody. Of course, this only lasts a few hours at best, and then it feels like a bad hangover and you begin to miss the other person. You might even start doing the silly things love makes you do, like leaving long texts and then deleting them before they're read, then resending them with some minor (or major) changes. Sometimes, you wish for the husband to realize his fault, so that things can go back to normal.

Well, I was having one of those days when I took the test again. Just when I was beginning to feel that these tests do not work, I saw two pink lines for the first time. I couldn't believe my eyes and called for another test, which showed the same results. I went to a doctor and triple checked this news before deciding my next course of action with my dear husband who, I imagined, was at that moment listing out the things that we both needed to divide among ourselves when the divorce came through.

Being Pregnant: The Facts and Myths

I later came to know that nothing of this sort had been happening at his end. He came back home with a big bouquet of flowers in one hand and a huge teddy bear in the other in an endeavour to make up for the fight. Little did he know that I would have a far better gift to give him. I took out a neatly gift-wrapped pregnancy test. One look at him and I knew life would never be the same again, and it was officially time to say goodbye to those childish fights forever.

The mix of feelings that a mother-to-be and a father-to-be go through are not the only emotions that are felt during a pregnancy. There are also the feelings of the people who are close to the new parents. These are feelings of responsibility, superior knowledge, experience, authority and the motherly urge to look after the parents-to-be, sometimes when there is no apparent need. Some of these strong emotions make it increasingly difficult for the mother-to-be. I have often wondered if the advice that some well-meaning people impart has any credibility or if it is a bid to prove themselves as more knowledgable.

There are many myths that prevail regarding pregnancy, depending on region or ethnicity. In India, it is believed that an expectant mother must shun Chinese food. In China, that is their staple diet! There is a Mexican superstition that if a pregnant woman looks at an eclipse, her unborn child's face would be bitten. In Israel, it is believed that if you have a food craving and you don't fulfil it, and you scratch yourself, your child will be born with a birthmark in the shape of the food you were craving. Many Indians believe that having a preference for a certain type of food (salty or sweet) while pregnant indicates the gender of the baby.

It cannot be determined why a particular myth begins and why such strange theories gain so much currency. I am going to share a few pregnancy-related myths that I busted through my research and experience.

I remember being petrified this one time I was taking a walk in my building compound. I had been trying to take care of my physical activity for the day, without a worry in the world. I was gently caressing my belly, something I absolutely loved to do, when an experienced mother walked up to me, looked me deep in the eyes as if trying hard to make a point, and then slowly uttered the most scary words that I have ever heard, '*Tight kapde pehenne se bacche ka dum ghut jata hai aur woh…* (Wearing tight clothes can suffocate the baby and…).' She waited for this to sink in, letting me complete the rest of the sentence in my head. I was dumbfounded! I was wearing extremely comfortable pregnancy workout clothes; they were so comfortable that I sometimes forgot what I was wearing. I suddenly saw them in a new light: were they really murderous, child-killing tools of doom?

There are many such myths related to dressing that I came across during my two pregnancies. The first myth, like I said, is that wearing tight clothes can suffocate the baby or stop the baby from growing within the womb. This is absolutely not true. The baby is safely protected inside the amniotic sac and has no contact with the clothes that we wear. After speaking to numerous OB-GYNs, including my own, and reading articles related to pregnancy dressing, I came to the conclusion that as long as I was comfortable, everything was fine. If I felt that a certain piece of clothing was making me uncomfortable, it was time to graduate to the next size or simply change. Pregnancy is not the time to hold on to clothes that have sentimental value. In fact, it is the time to splurge if you're into that sort of thing because your size does change fast and so does the definition of comfortable clothes.

Another interesting but obviously untrue myth that I

came across was that if my humongous baby bump could be seen through my clothes then my baby was at a huge risk of catching the evil eye. This frankly sounded ridiculous to me, like an old wives' tale. How is one supposed to conceal the baby bump? It's not as if any shapewear available in the market has been especially designed for a baby bump! And, even if there is, why would I want to conceal the bump and deprive myself of the amazing treatment a pregnant woman receives?

Another strange myth I encountered was when hundreds of people messaged me on social media, enquiring how I was wearing jeans while pregnant. I was reprimanded for being a careless mother who was only concerned about fashion and looking good while completely disregarding her unborn child's well-being. Everybody seemed to care more about my child than me. I would like to take this opportunity to educate both the pregnant mothers reading this and the people who worry about pregnant mothers' dressing that there are numerous apparel brands that make maternity clothes. These clothes are specially designed for pregnant mothers. They are made with a lot of care and they make you look and feel absolutely gorgeous! Among these wonderful outfits are extremely comfortable maternity jeans, which have a soft, stretchable cotton waistband that can accommodate your belly no matter how big it gets. I practically lived in the same pair of maternity jeans right from the third month to the day I delivered. There are many pregnant mothers who choose to wear loose-fitted clothes. Some like to hide their belly and others, like me, prefer to show it off. I even knew a mother who was so unbothered that she once, by mistake, wore a kurti inside out to the mall and after this was pointed out to her, she refrained from changing and simply said, 'I'm pregnant, when else can I wear something inside out?' I believe that pregnancy fashion, just like any other kind of fashion, is a completely personal choice. Every mother should have the free will to decide what kind of clothes she wants to wear to make herself comfortable and to make her pregnancy memorable, without worrying about whether her choice of clothes will be detrimental to the baby's health.

Can the same, however, be said about the activities pregnant women do in a day? While I was applauded for continuing to work until I went into labour, I also got a lot of flak from many. I still fail to understand the brouhaha over it. I was told by at least one person every day that I should be resting, that I should stop working and stop going to office because I was pregnant. Some others decided to simply gossip among themselves and did not wish to make their judgements evident. The only person other than me that did not seem to have any problem was my doctor. I thoroughly enjoyed going to office every day because it took my mind off things. I also felt much calmer when I was busy working and I honestly never thought about my pregnancy as something that was supposed to change my beautiful daily routine.

As it turns out, and I wonder why this is something that nobody realizes, every pregnancy is different. I had an extremely healthy pregnancy and hence was able to continue most activities normally. Although it could also be the other way around. Perhaps, I had a perfectly healthy pregnancy *because* I continued to do most activities normally. Some mothers experience special circumstances that lead them to take special precautions while they're pregnant. These circumstances may include issues like in vitro fertilization, gestational diabetes, high blood pressure, iron deficiency, excess weight gain, decreased amniotic fluid and morning sickness, among others. Whether a pregnant mother should continue to work also depends on factors like the kind of hours or efforts she is required to put in. Is she required to stand for long hours, which can cause discomfort? Is she required to do a lot of physical activity, like riding a bicycle? Is she required to travel long distances in local trains or auto rickshaws, and be at crowded railway stations or bus stops? Does she end up going long hours without food? Is her work very stressful or have odd hours?

So, basically, every time I was told by a well-meaning intruder to go home and rest, I smiled and continued my work. My advice to all pregnant mothers would be to take no one's advice (not even mine) except your doctor's when it comes to deciding whether to continue working during your pregnancy. But definitely take my advice and do what I did the next time somebody tells you to rest it out when your doctor has already given you the nod to work.

While how you feel doing a certain activity is something only you know best, it is a completely different story when it comes to eating. What *you* eat is directly consumed by the baby through the amniotic fluid. Naturally then, there are many foods, like coffee, that are frowned upon and labelled 'not to be consumed by a pregnant woman'. I am a huge coffee addict and it, in a way, determines my mood. Happiness is equal to coffee and the lack of it leads to a cranky mood. How was I able to control my pregnancy mood swings without my regular dose of caffeine then? Caffeine, as I learnt to my disappointment, is not a pregnant mother's best friend. It can have serious side effects if overdone. During my first pregnancy, I shunned everything that remotely had caffeine in it, starting with coffee, be it tiramisu, tea, certain ice-creams, caffeinated soft drinks, caffeinated candies and many others.

In the fifth month of my first pregnancy, I woke up one morning and looked at my husband having his morning tea. I remember that sight made me so sad that I broke down. I kept crying and Mohit couldn't help wondering whether it was because of something he did! I went and sat on his lap and admitted that I was extremely sad because all I wanted was to eat a sugary biscuit with a hot cup of ginger tea. 'Is it really so bad to be pregnant? Can I not even fulfil this simplest of desires?' He looked at me in awe and reminded me that my doctor had never stopped me from having tea. And I reminded him that tea had caffeine in it. That was the day I realized that being a happy pregnant woman is far more important than being a decaffeinated one.

I fixed an appointment with my OB-GYN the very same day to discuss this high priority issue. She looked at my face and literally begged me to have two cups of tea every day! It was like a prescription coming from her. I remember walking out of her room with a big smile on my face.

Having tasted blood, during my second pregnancy, I wanted something stronger. Tea was not going to cut it for me this time, so I went looking for better answers. This time, my doctor told me that up to 200 mg caffeine in a day is perfectly safe for the baby and that if I still felt apprehensive, I could increase my water intake by two glasses per cup of coffee consumed, which I did. Additionally, I patted my back for a really smart thing I did. Not only did I switch to a decaffeinated version, which has only 20–30 mg caffeine per serving, compared to the 200 mg in regular coffee, I also slowly reduced the amount of coffee I put in one cup of black brew and brought it down to one-third the amount I was otherwise having in a cup. Basically, I could have three cups a day but still consumed only 30 mg caffeine. I also got really popular in all the neighbouring coffee shops, since my cravings for non-homemade cold coffee increased. Every time they saw me walking in with my big baby bump, huffing and puffing but never failing to pick up my favourite cold beverage, they knew exactly what they had to do. They would make my customized coffee with only half the shot of coffee and no sugar. I sometimes feel that they stopped recognizing me on purpose and took it personally when I went back to those cafes sans the bump and the special order—almost as if they sulked at being asked to make the 'regular' cold coffee! Besides caffeine, there were a few other things for which I was frowned upon. More about that in the chapter about my pregnancy and post-partum diet.

For now, I would like nothing more than to take you through some lighter moments from my pregnancy where I heard things about myself and my baby that were so outrageous that I was left tongue-tied. At the risk of sounding pompous, I must admit that there has rarely ever been a time that I haven't thought of something smart to say in any given situation. In the hotter months of my first pregnancy, which were pretty much all of my pregnancy because it is always hot in Mumbai and more so if you're pregnant, I preferred going for my evening walks after

Being Pregnant: The Facts and Myths

sunset. In the garden area of my apartment building, there was an unlit, dark corner. One day, I overheard a conversation between a few ladies and some kids playing. They said that a snake had been seen in that dark corner a few days ago and hence it was not advisable for the kids to go and play there. Naturally, I was worried, too, since, let's face it, who wants to be bitten by a snake, especially when pregnant? I got curious and asked those ladies if that was really true or just something they made up, so the kids would go home. Those ladies gave me an interesting aside (if only it were true), apparently about pregnant mothers across the world. '*Aap walk kar lo. Aap toh pregnant ho. Aapko saanp nahi katega* (You may continue walking since you're pregnant. The snake won't bite you).' They, then, casually walked away, leaving me in that dark corner where, in my imagination, a deadly snake lurked waiting to bite a woman, any woman, pregnant or otherwise. Needless to say, I did not go back to take a walk in that particular corner of the garden! Well, I wasn't going to bust a myth of that magnitude by being brave and proving that a snake might just bite a pregnant woman! No ladies, I'd rather be smart than brave. My advice: you too be smart and avoid gardens with notoriously harmless reptiles. Don't blame me later saying I didn't warn you!

Then there were the less-entertaining escapades where I was told to not drink tea—not because it has caffeine, but because my baby would be born dark-skinned if I had tea. Had the caffeine in the tea not bothered me, I swear I would have had a tad too much of the beverage in anticipation of having a dark- and shiny-skinned baby! First, if that sort of thing bothers you, let me clarify, tea will not be a deciding factor in the colour of your baby's skin tone. Second, and more importantly, there is nothing wrong with brown skin. In fact, I love it and I am proud to be brown skinned myself! Thankfully, I did not have to call my doctor to know that our baby's skin tone had already been decided, thanks to the genes that Mohit and I blessed him/her with. I might add that consuming coconut water every day will not give you a fair baby, although it will give you a lot of other health benefits. I regularly had coconut water and will detail this in the chapter about my pregnancy diet.

There is another interesting thing to ponder over: the myth that if a pregnant woman catches a whiff of a delicious meal being cooked in someone's house, it is imperative that she stops, rings their bell and asks them to let her have a taste. It is irrelevant whether she knows them or whether it is a socially acceptable thing to do. All that matters is that if she craves to eat that particular food and deprives herself of it, thus depriving the baby, he or she will be drooling for a year after birth. Ever seen babies with drool trickling down their chins at all times? Sounds like most babies? Now you know that they do this because their mothers did not give in to a certain craving! For the record, this is one of my favourite pregnancy related myths because I just can't help picturing pregnant women lining up outside random houses, demanding they be allowed to taste the delicious smelling food being cooked in their kitchens.

You may have also heard that travelling is not advisable when you're pregnant. This rule should be followed only if your doctor says it is! In fact, in the first trimester, I travelled to Kasauli in one of the most eventful journeys of my life. We had an upcoming web series on one of my YouTube channels with multiple brand partners on board, and this required us to travel to the hills to meet the demands of our location partners. The brave soul that I am, I decided that I was not going to renege on my commitment just because I was pregnant. Besides, as per the plan, it was a one-day journey to the place, six days of shoot, a day's return journey and that's it! Sounds simple enough, right? That's exactly why I said yes to it, though it did not turn out anything like that. We took a flight from Mumbai to New Delhi and then from New Delhi to Chandigarh. But in the flight to Chandigarh, the captain announced that since the visibility in Chandigarh was zero, we would be returning to New Delhi airport. So, I and the whole crew circled back to Delhi, and now we had no other choice but to book a bus to travel to Kasauli by road. However, this was not the end of my misery, for the bus took way too long to arrive and we had to walk with our suitcases literally on our heads running from the airport to the bus stop where our private bus was to arrive. The journey was extremely uncomfortable, but I kept hoping for the light at the end of the tunnel. That was until we reached a place in the middle of nowhere where there had been a landslide, causing a massive traffic jam! Now my worry was not whether we would reach our destination the same night, but merely where I was going to pee in this traffic jam, since we all know how badly the bladder gets pressurized while you're pregnant. By then, night

Being Pregnant: The Facts and Myths

had fallen, and I could not sit any longer. I desperately needed a bed and some cozy blankets to sleep. Once we got out of the traffic jam, I instructed my production team to find a decent hotel and book us all in for the night. I can only imagine how they must have sworn under their breaths wondering what an unreasonable, not to mention expensive, demand the lady had! They gave in eventually because, at the end of the day, it was my money that was being spent. Finally, it was only the next morning that we reached our destination in Kasauli. The return journey was no less adventurous. The whole week saw Murphy's Law in action, from air travel, road travel, train travel, landslides, diversions, torrential rains, cancelled flights, etc. All of these are things you are not supposed to do when you're pregnant, right?

There are risks involved at every point, with the biggest risk being a miscarriage. At this point, thankfully, there were no eyebrows raised, since nobody knew I was pregnant, or a barrage of concerning (read: judgemental) statements would have followed. I just kept going fearlessly. The only thing I followed was the simple connection that I had made with my body. It was my friend and guide. The mind–body connection and the simple rule

I had—I sat when I got tired and stood up again when I felt rested—kept me going. In hindsight, I may have got my strength because my superpowers had doubled, now that I was going to be a mother once again! What other explanation could there have been for shooting a swimming pool sequence in a hill station, amidst rain, while running a fever, which I did most days in the first trimester, and feeling fine to continue for the rest of the days? I would be doing all this without even getting the regular five-star treatment that a pregnant mother gets because nobody knew! Not once did my body tell me to stop or I would have. It was only two months later when I announced my pregnancy that all my crew members forgave me with all their hearts for all the little tantrums I had thrown.

Did any of you, perchance, wonder why I did not tell anyone about the pregnancy? That is another myth surrounding a pregnancy, that one should not announce it to the world for the first three months. It is believed that this could cause a miscarriage and the expecting mother should do all she can to hide it. While I personally don't believe in myths in general, this one has a special place in my heart. The first three months of both my pregnancies were like a secret that I shared with my husband, and nobody knew about it even though there were people around us all the time. The secret looks we stole, the silent way he cared for my little needs—like getting a bathroom cleaned for me, fetching a bottle of water, a chair, letting me sleep in a bit extra in the mornings while he woke up early for shoots, these were all priceless moments. This might even have made people gossip about how I was getting star treatment just because I was the producer or director's wife.

These moments took me back to my very first shoot when I faced the camera as an actor for the first time, and my romance with Mohit had just started blossoming. The little finger that would glide across my back, or the meaningful look that he would give me from under the cap he would always wear on the sets those days. The first trimester felt pretty much like that. It was like sharing a moment just between the two of us. Sometimes, I wish I could get pregnant just to experience that love again. Perhaps that's an exaggeration, but I hope you get the gist. I guess this could be the reason why the *bade buzurg* (elderly) say that a couple can almost save their failing marriage if they get pregnant. The bond that it creates between a couple is not just special but truly strong.

If romance is not a strong enough reason for you, scientifically also, the first three months are crucial for a successful pregnancy. Since the foetus is still developing and needs to form a better connection with the mother's body, it may be a safer option to let nature takes its course before you announce the pregnancy to the world. That way, in case you suffer an early miscarriage, which is not uncommon to be honest, you don't have to announce to the world that it didn't work out this time. This is a myth I like to believe in because it is not entirely without logic.

In retrospect, these popular myths led to some of the quaint events that made my pregnancies memorable. All said and done, what is most important is to stay calm when you're pregnant. There is no point in blindly believing what you hear from another person, whether it is a relative or a friend, because everybody has had their own experiences, and so will you. I personally chose to completely go against any form of well-meaning advice I got. The reason for doing this was not defiance because that would have meant I was arrogant and even stupid. I did this because at every stage in my pregnancy, I always took the advice of the relevant person—a person who actually had the domain knowledge related to the particular topic. Would you go to an investment banker and ask her if turmeric needs to be added to the butter chicken before or after the tomatoes go in, even if the investment banker had cooked butter chicken the previous week and hence would know the answer? Why then would you take pregnancy advice from your best friend who, even though she may love you a lot, may not really have the necessary expertise? The chances of her pregnancy being different from yours in at least some ways would be close to a hundred per cent. For that reason, my go-to person was my doctor in most cases, and my very own body in others.

So, if you're pregnant or are planning to be, rest assured you will come across many such judgements, myths or advice as you progress. The majority of it will be the outcome of genuine love and concern and you must appreciate it for that reason, rather than taking it to heart. One thing that you should always remember is that pregnancy is one of the most beautiful phases of a woman's life and in no way should it be treated like an illness. It is a time to look after yourself, pamper yourself and be truly happy. Whether you choose to work or stay at home, work out, relax or spend a lot of time with yourself, streamlining your thoughts and connecting with yourself, you most certainly should start preparing yourself for the baby to come, physically and mentally.

Talking about preparation, I went ahead and broke another stereotype. I continued to do weightlifting and even continued to run while I was pregnant. Read on to know my workout routine during my pregnancy.

3

Developing the Mind–Body Connection

Fitness to me is a lot like knowing the right time to have a baby. It is subjective, it is personal and it is important for a mother's growth. It informs a mother's self-esteem, emotional health and physical health. It can make or break post-partum health if it is not prioritized or is done at the wrong time, too soon or too late. It cannot be based on drawing parallels with others. It needs to define the starting point of a mother's journey and go upwards from there. It is also not restricted to physicality but is a holistic way of life. It does not have a mantra but is, in fact, a journey to self-discovery. It was one of the most amazing journeys that I began after I became a mother.

While I may have started on the road to fitness after I had Areeza, I found the path to be so therapeutic that I continued to move forward even when I was carrying Arham. It is commonly believed that pregnancy is the time to slow down, switch to yoga and meditation, take slow gentle walks, so on and so forth. It is absolutely right to do all those things. I practised yoga when I was pregnant the first time and took relaxing walks every day. But let me tell you, I chose to do that during my first pregnancy because it was right for me then. I decided to choose other methods to maintain my fitness during my second pregnancy because, by that time, those were the right choices for me. For some expecting mothers, swimming is the first choice while for others, it may be running. What suits you best depends on how your lifestyle has been before you get pregnant. Pregnancy should not be a reason to completely alter your lifestyle. However, little adjustments here and there will make all the difference.

When I got pregnant the first time, I was 31, and

Developing the Mind–Body Connection

had never been inside a gym. Naturally, I wasn't going to start experimenting with my body while I was pregnant, and that is not something I would advise any pregnant mother to do either. But continuing to do what you have been doing for years before you even considered getting pregnant is definitely safe, if you continue to keep your healthcare provider in the loop at every step.

I am aware that mothers get really worried about the baby's health while performing any kind of activity and that is completely fair. In fact, the baby is not the only person you should worry about. How we live during our pregnancy can have a lifelong impact on our own health as well. I remember being petrified the first time I performed simple yoga asanas, even though I was under the care and guidance of a certified maternity yoga practitioner. In my class of about ten pregnant women, I was the only one who would refuse to lie on her back while performing the shava asana. I had read somewhere that lying on your back could be unsafe during pregnancy, since that particular position puts the weight of the growing uterus on the vena cava, which is a large vein that provides blood to your heart and back; this basically means that you and your baby's lives are at risk in that position. While this is true, it is also true that this is only an issue after the fifth month or so, and even then, it does not pose any threat if it is done for a few minutes. But when you're pregnant, there's no convincing you about certain things that you believe are true, and this is one of the first signs you should start to read your own body. In my experience, when you don't feel right about something, it is usually not right for you. When you feel right about something, you should stop worrying about what others might say or how they might react and just listen to your body. The only person whose opinion should matter is your healthcare provider. From refusing to lie down on my back in the first pregnancy to doing crunches and even running during my second was not an easy shift, though it was also not a deliberate one.

It started with my first post-partum weight loss journey. Since I had never had serious weight issues prior to my first pregnancy, I had no experience in weight loss or diets. It was good for me in a way because that way I got to learn everything my way and customized it for my body. A little look around me and I realized that when it comes to weight loss, the good old gym offers the best options. Slowly but surely, I started learning weight training. I combined this with running and tried my hand at skipping, and then experimented with various combinations of everything I had learnt. Since I was carefully monitoring my inch and weight loss, I naturally started observing the changes I felt in my body. How much weight was enough for me to lift in different exercises; how many sets per exercise were giving me just enough soreness to feel the burn but not fatigue; how many days I needed between working out each body part to maintain the burn and not overdo it—these were some of things that became a natural part of my observation.

Every time I would observe somebody performing an exercise that seemed new to me, I would make a mental note of it, go back home and research that exercise. But if I didn't feel comfortable after trying my hand at that exercise, I would simply not do it. Soon, I realized that it was time I hired a professional fitness trainer to teach me the right form because there was so much to learn. When you are weight training, correct form and technique are crucial to avoid any injuries, especially for a beginner like I was at the time. It is important to add here that while your activity and lifestyle during pregnancy will have a lifelong impact on you, they will also be extremely important post-partum, since this is the time your body is healing while also getting accustomed to the new way of life.

I have always been a dedicated and a quick learner and it helped me develop my own programmes to fit my needs. It took me steady hard work of about 12–15 months to lose all my pregnancy weight and get into the best shape that I had ever been in until then. I had lost 10 kg in the most healthy way. Although my fitness goal had been achieved, I was so addicted to my workouts that I could never stop being fit. Being fit, in fact, had a whole new meaning now. It was not about 'losing weight' anymore; it was about feeling fit and healthy from within. It was a way of life. Recognizing my own body, reading the signals it was sending me, building my stamina, getting out of my comfort zone and knowing when to do so, are some of the things that make me feel the most alive.

Naturally then, when I got pregnant the second time, I did not see any reason to stop doing what my body had got so used to over six years of training. But when I started sharing my pregnancy workout videos on social media, I was brutally judged and trolled, although weightlifting for pregnant mothers is much more common and not so frowned upon in many other countries. This

Developing the Mind–Body Connection

is purely because a vast majority of pregnant mothers in India have never been into weightlifting even before they got pregnant and because there are a lot of myths surrounding weight training for pregnant mothers. Let's look at those before moving forward.

It is believed that pregnant mothers should not let their heart rate increase beyond a point and weightlifting can cause a sudden increase in the heart rate. This brings a very vivid image to my mind. I see a big-built man lifting 150 pounds of massive looking weights on a barbell and doing crazy deadlifts. I can almost hear him scream and pant. Now I replace this man with a big-built pregnant woman! Of course, that is a scary image, but it is also an image that is fictitious and a figment of my wild imagination. While pregnancy is no time to break records or set new ones for yourself, it is also a proven fact that working out every day will make the pregnancy and childbirth experience smoother. Hence, just let your doctor decide for you whether you are fit to work out and, if yes, how much of it is good for you and what kind of exercise is best suited for you as per *your* preference.

It is also believed that overheating and dehydration is unavoidable while lifting weights. It is true that overheating can cause neural tube defects, especially during the first trimester, but it is also true that avoiding overheating is actually quite easy, especially if, like me, weight training is the route you choose. While lifting moderate weights, in an airconditioned gym, the chances of overheating are pretty slim. A good way to determine how high your heart rate is and whether you're hitting the danger zone is by allowing yourself to make small talk with others around you. If you can carry on a conversation, you should be absolutely fine. In fact, during my pregnancy, I made more friends than ever before in the gym since I found this to be not just a good practice to check my heart rate and exhaustion levels but I also felt protected being surrounded by friendly faces.

The other thing that most expecting mothers fear is that going to the gym will make them feel even more exhausted and tired than they already do. Yes, I know how we need to hold on to every ounce of extra energy that we have. But in my experience, the more you train your body, the less exhausted you will feel. This is stamina building. During pregnancy, on the days I put in an effort to accomplish moderate exercise, I felt far more energetic than on the days I did not. Needless to say, you may feel

Developing the Mind–Body Connection

differently on different days and if putting in an effort feels like too much on a certain day, that is the day your body does need the rest. At least that is the mantra I swore by. How I adjusted to the pregnancy in the gym is something I will elaborate on at length because, as my pregnancy progressed, that is what most people started to recognize me as—the weightlifting pregnant mama.

I was heavily reprimanded for doing deadlifts with a bump, but I firmly believe the one thing that kept me going, actually leading to a very healthy pregnancy, was the fact that I continued to workout throughout my pregnancy. I could have chosen yoga, like I did in my first pregnancy, but yoga was not going to cut it for me this time around because my body was accustomed to much more high intensity workouts. I felt centred in a gym. Leaving weight training would have meant doing something out of my comfort zone and pregnancy is not the time to test your limits. Many mothers would feel going to the gym is getting out of their comfort zone and I reiterate that if that is how you feel then indeed a gym is not for you when you're pregnant. I felt absolutely at ease when I worked out. I felt calm and rejuvenated in the gym; my breath was rhythmic and I could regulate my heart rate in my own comfort zone. I could also monitor my body heat levels much better when indoors in an airconditioned room and could decide my own pace. I couldn't find any reason to quit doing what I loved just because I was pregnant. If anything, being pregnant means actually doing the things that you love which you otherwise probably cannot. So, while some mothers may indulge in savouries and watching a lot of films and television or simply enjoy their resting phase, others can very well choose to go to the gym.

When I decided to continue weight training, I asked my healthcare provider if it was alright; although I felt fine, I hoped I was not being stupid or putting myself and my baby at risk. There was absolutely no hesitation when she told me to continue everything that I did unless I felt uncomfortable doing it. Squats, lunges, chest presses, barbell rows, even deadlifts—I continued every single thing and only thought of one thing while working out: am I feeling comfortable? Every time the answer was in the affirmative, I knew I was on the right path. I think it is fair to say that lifting weights has taught me, in the true sense, how to understand my own body. I practise being completely in sync with my body while lifting weights. What other way is there? If you lose that connection, you can hurt yourself: be it in the gym or in life. That's how I built the mind–body connection, where I felt every sensation within my body mindfully. Would you believe it if I told you that I could actually tell when I had conceived the second time?

We had been trying for three months and it was disappointing to discover every month that I'd have to wait another month to find out if there was good news. The mothers who go through this disappointment for several months know what I'm talking about. Sex becomes a very responsible and calculated thing to do. You have to time it, and after you've done this whole exercise while you are ovulating, you have to remember to take the test on the day you are expecting your menstrual cycle to begin. I invariably ended up taking the test too soon only to find that it was negative yet again.

When I actually conceived, I knew I didn't have to take the pregnancy test. It was a weird feeling I got in the stomach in the middle of my cycle, similar to menstruating, but much stronger. My breasts felt tender and extremely sensitive and not in a sexual way. I felt more tired than usual, and gym started to feel like a burden. It felt like deja vu. I remembered feeling this way when I had been pregnant the first time, except at that time I had not recognized this very loud signal that my body had been giving me. This time, though, I recognized those signs and decided to take a break from everything for three weeks. The body is working overtime creating that little pea-sized baby in the first month. I let my body work and gave it the rest it asked for. Once the news was confirmed, around the fifth week, I went to the doctor and got a green light to get back to the gym.

In the following months, I made my peace with being the centre of attention in the gym as the crazy lady with the bump. I even had a person remark that I may end up miscarrying right there in the gym! '*Ye aurat pagal ho gayi hai, baccha gir jayega tab samajh mein aayega kya* (This woman has gone crazy. Will she only learn a lesson if she drops the baby)?' There were also some genuinely concerned people glaring at me who were standing on their marks, in position, to catch a dumb-bell, or me, or the baby, depending on which fell first. Silently enjoying the attention that I knew would last only a few months, I continued everything like nothing had happened; the only difference being that when my body told me to sit,

I sat and got up only when my body felt ready. Since this kind of surreal connection that I felt with my body was built in the gym, it felt reasonable to continue it now and make it stronger.

Workout During the First Trimester

The first trimester is the most crucial time because this is when the baby is establishing a connection with your body to sustain itself. Like I mentioned, I stopped all activity/workouts from the second to the fifth week, until my pregnancy was confirmed and my doctor gave me the nod to hit the gym again. Even then, there were days when getting out of bed seemed like a burden, and I stayed in bed for a couple of hours extra before hitting the gym. Once back in the gym, I started lifting lighter weights than usual and slowly built my strength back up by the time I was in my third month. I worked out five days a week for one hour each. I did mild cardio twice a week, which included interval training by alternating between running for one minute and walking for 30 seconds. I kept this routine flexible, increased the recovery (walking) time and decreased the running time on occasions, not going above the speed of 8 kmph at any given point of time. I usually ran for around 30–45 minutes depending on my stamina on that day.

The rest of the days were dedicated to weight training—one day for chest and biceps, one day for lower body, a day for back and triceps and a day for shoulders. Many times, I alternated the exercise of a particular body part and did not follow a set pattern. For example, the day I felt too tired to do legs, I would simply switch to arms instead even if it was supposed to be leg day. The arm is a smaller muscle and is less exhausting for me. I did basic crunches every day, but took care to not hold my stomach tight and not crunch too much to avoid any kind of pressure on the abdomen.

Different mothers may feel very differently during the crucial first trimester and it is of utmost importance that whatever activity you choose for yourself is totally in tandem with the advice given by your healthcare provider.

Workout During the Second Trimester

I checked with my OB-GYN at every single visit and told her in detail about the exercises I did and if she told me

Developing the Mind–Body Connection

to refrain from anything, I didn't argue. Barring skipping, I don't remember any exercise that she told me to avoid. The second trimester was my most active trimester, as is with most mothers. I felt that my huffing and puffing had reduced and I was able to do more repetitions in each set. By now I even increased the weight I was lifting in each exercise and felt absolutely comfortable while doing so. The thing about weights is that there are only so many ways you can make your workout more intense. For example, do more repetitions that would give you different results or increase the amount of weight you lift while making the number of repetitions lesser. I chose to be somewhere in the middle. I would lift the amount of weight that would allow me to do 12–15 repetitions comfortably without making me pant. I was more productive in office and was able to run around with Areeza much more too. I almost felt normal. I gradually reduced my running duration down to 10 minutes, and made it more of a brisk walk. I did this because the size of my uterus was increasing and the thudding sound started to make me uncomfortable. While many pregnant mothers run till the eighth month, I was not going to make any benchmarks for myself. This was me reading the signs of my own body.

Around the fifth month, I started swimming regularly. Now my five-day workout week looked like this: three days of weight training, a day of swimming and a day of running/brisk walking. When I swam, I did 45–50 minutes of non-stop swimming, swiftly alternating between the strokes. I gradually discontinued crunches because there was hardly any distinct upper abdomen left for me to perform the exercise for.

This is also a time when doctors advise you to take your last trip before you have the baby, often called the 'babymoon'. Mohit took me to Hong Kong and my workout sessions gave way to a lot of walking around the city during those 10 days. I remember starting to feel a slight pain near my groin and I would frequently sit down before resuming again. Later, when I came back to Mumbai, my OB-GYN educated me that it was due to the growing pressure the uterus was putting on the nerves surrounding that area and that rest was the only thing that would help at that point because it relieves the pressure for the time being. It was very interesting to note that the only discomfort I felt was due to walking, which is undoubtedly the most popular exercise for pregnant women around the globe. On the other hand,

Developing the Mind–Body Connection

I absolutely never felt any discomfort in working out at the gym, which is looked down upon by most as the least common fitness regime for pregnant mothers. Could this be because I was doing something my body was more used to—lifting weights than walking? Why don't you go ahead and answer that for yourself, and the answer will help you determine what is best suited for you when you are pregnant.

When you're pregnant, every day feels different at times. Your mood, energy levels, stamina and enthusiasm may have dips and highs. It is extremely important to factor this in. While you may have a tentative plan for the day, you should also change plans as your stamina or mood changes. My second trimester was also the time we bought a new house and I was extremely busy getting the interior work done. Naturally, I had to stand on my feet for long hours, and my mind was working overtime thinking about things like setting up Areeza's room, getting the nursery ready, getting the kitchen functional, etc. I did not want to move in *after* the baby's arrival, since I knew that it was going to be really hard to plan these things post-partum, considering my body would need to heal and my mind would need to be peaceful, relaxed and rested.

All this required a lot more energy than a pregnant lady has to dispense. So, there were many days that I woke up feeling fatigued and altered my workout accordingly.

Workout During Third Trimester

By the time my seventh month was over, I completely stopped running and switched to brisk walks. I did increase the duration to 60 minutes to compensate for the decrease in cardio, but stopped like a good little girl and went back home if I felt the pressure around the groin area returning. Do you know the importance of cardio in our lives? I feel that somehow cardiovascular exercises don't get their due in the weightlifting world. But if you ask me, stamina building cannot happen if you do not exercise the most important organ of your body: the heart. Why do some people start panting after the same amount of activity while others don't? It is stamina, right? And hence, I always attached importance to my weekly cardio, even when I was pregnant because I knew the importance of stamina during pregnancy. Let me remind you once again that pregnancy cardio was nothing like the cardio I did after my delivery because, like I said, pregnancy is

Developing the Mind–Body Connection

no time to set new records. A mild increase in the heart rate is what you should work towards.

I continued my exercise regime with a daily breakdown similar to my second trimester, which included swimming. I swam practically till the day I delivered because it brought me an inexplicable amount of peace. The rhythmic motion produced a sound that was no less than music. The pool continues to also be the place where I automatically disconnect from everything else around me, be it people or mobile phones and other gadgets, and just purely connect with myself and my body. It is also a time when one doesn't even listen to music and hence is a great way to purify and rest the mind. It is an excellent exercise for everybody, pregnant or not. The weight training stopped when I entered the tenth month with no signs of the baby yet. I had grown too huge to do anything other than walk. Even the walking reduced to barely 20 minutes and that too holding Mohit's hand, since my feet had swollen up way too much. In fact, I could not even perform the much-needed duck walks at this time, which my doctor had strongly advised me to do! Cutely enough, my daughter Areeza, who was six years old at the time, did the duck walks with me, trying to help me balance.

It made me feel quite overwhelmed, imagining how this little angel will be towards the new arrival!

Let me narrate a little anecdote here. When I was in the tenth month and found it a struggle to even walk, I had a nagging pain in my left foot. I showed it to my doctor and, as anybody would, she also told me that it is pregnancy-related and once the swelling settles, so will the pain. However, the pain continued till about a month after the delivery and slowly faded away. I don't remember when exactly, since my mind was by then too occupied with the new arrival's troubles to focus on my own. It was much later that we discovered that I had had a fracture of the fourth metatarsal and that was the reason why walking had become a struggle. For the life of me, I cannot remember what could have caused the fracture; it may have happened during one of my foot massage sessions when my therapist insisted he could take out all the swelling in a day, even though I repeatedly reminded him this was not water retention or tiredness related swelling, but swelling related to pregnancy, which takes its own time to go away. Well, I kept myself calm by telling myself that he had only been trying to help. But how it happened is not something I like to focus

Developing the Mind–Body Connection

on, since, really, how does it even matter anymore? Look on the bright side! There I was, full-blown nine months pregnant, with a belly the size of a small hillock, feet swollen up, running around getting my house work done, office work and and to think that I was doing all of that with a fractured foot! Imagine the kind of strength a woman, especially a mother, has within her. Once we set our minds on something, there's no stopping us. Take a moment to close your eyes and tell yourself how amazingly strong you are!

My estimated due date was 4 May and my water finally broke on 12 May after I went down for a long walk in the garden with Mohit. This was one of the most memorable walks of my pregnancy, of course primarily because my water broke soon after. It was also memorable because I remember almost crying in discomfort, clutching on to Mohit's hand, almost leaning on him to walk and having a very emotional talk with my baby inside the womb, requesting him to come out now. Mohit and I had opted for hypnobirthing and were avoiding any medical interference till the time the doctor reassured us that everything was safe. This day was also special because it was Mother's Day and, as if magically, Arham chose this day to come into this world and make me a mother again. I finally delivered on 13 May.

Thanks to the continuous exercise I did throughout my pregnancy, I was able to stay on my feet (even though one of them was fractured!) throughout. It also helped avoid the common complications that mothers experience due to excessive weight gain. But weight gain should not be the reason to work out during your pregnancy if you do choose to go down that road. The real reason is to stay fit and healthy and be able to carry a healthy baby inside you. And while it is sometimes important to push yourself, it is also extremely important to realize your own limits, because pregnancy is no time to push them. The safest thing to do is always keep your healthcare provider in the loop about whatever it is you're planning to do for your fitness. Never hesitate to schedule an extra appointment to discuss your health and fitness. I gained roughly 17 kg during my pregnancy and most of it was concentrated around the abdomen. I also found it extremely easy to lose the weight once I delivered the baby.

I know many of you are eager to read about my post-partum weight loss journey and I will share it in the chapters to come. Being fit has a new meaning once you

Developing the Mind–Body Connection

become a mother, and it is wiser to realize its importance gradually, as nature allows you the time, rather than all of a sudden. It is possible, mind you, to be in even better shape after the birth of your baby but not without hard work and taking smart, careful measures. But before we get into that, you must know that post-partum fitness or weight loss starts the day you get pregnant, *not* after you deliver. There are so many mothers who don't know this and wonder why it is so difficult to come back to their pre-pregnancy shape. For me, my fitness and diet took priority over everything else from the day I got pregnant. And as the popular proverb goes, 'You are what you eat,' so let's start by talking about what I ate and what I avoided during pregnancy. What you eat during your pregnancy will play a defining role in your post-partum health as well.

4

The Importance of Diet during Pregnancy

Why is being pregnant considered such an important phase of a woman's life? Why do people around a pregnant woman make her feel so important and special? Why do pregnant women need to be looked after even though they may be perfectly independent otherwise? There may be exceptions, but this is the general rule that everybody experiences. The most common reason for this is that the family of the pregnant mother is extremely excited about the new arrival

The Importance of Diet during Pregnancy

in the family and suddenly, everything starts centring around that new life getting ready, and since the mother is the medium to reach that life, she obviously becomes the centre of attention and the tender love and care of well-meaning family members. The other reason is the fact that a pregnant mother just looks so uncomfortable most of the time. Mind you, the focus here is on 'looks'. Although she may not necessarily feel so, it is enough to make the others around her offer her a chair or water or any other thing she might need at any given point in time.

The most important reason for this attention, in my opinion, is that the woman, who was so far concerned only with her immediate responsibilities or goals, is now suddenly responsible for a human life! To help the little one who is inside her womb, she is also responsible for bolstering her own health and safety now, since the baby will draw nutrition from the mother's abundant stores. This is how she realizes the importance of good health.

Have you ever noticed how teenagers eat? Or how college students eat—their diet or lifestyle? In fact, how was your own lifestyle when you were that age? I remember how I never ate breakfast when I was in senior school. It was just so 'cool' to reach school and eat at the canteen. Only the 'LS' kids or the 'unsmart', 'uncool' kids ate at home or brought the tiffins that had been carefully prepared and lovingly packed by their mothers. When I was in college, I freaked out on cafeteria food and why not? The Lady Shri Ram café was the coolest in the whole of South Campus: the kheema samosas, dal makhani, paranthas, Chinese food, everything was so delicious! And if, for any reason, I did not eat at the college cafeteria, there was always the nearby McDonald's at the Greater Kailash market. I felt so proud that I could eat two whole burgers along with fries and an aerated drink at the same time! At that age, neither weight gain nor ill health feels like an issue. Many of us almost never encounter a lifestyle disease at that age and hence we feel invincible. However, our mothers feel so concerned for our health and, no matter how smart we are, we never understand the reason for the concern till we become parents ourselves or have an encounter with a diet-related health issue. Once we become mothers ourselves, there is a complete shift in our outlook.

Becoming a mother is almost the same as having a second birth. That is because the new life that a mother lives is in no way similar to the one she was living before

The Importance of Diet during Pregnancy

she conceived. Also, if the mother is healthy, chances of the baby being healthy are higher. So, for me, every other reason is secondary. The health of the mother is of paramount importance—her physical health as well as mental health.

In some ways, you cannot separate physical health from mental health. If the diet is good, the mind will also be peaceful. If you are eating healthy, it will ensure happy messages are imparted from the body to the mind. If you are staying away from junk, your cravings will reduce drastically till they completely vanish. If you are avoiding processed sugar, the insulin balance of your body will ensure a happy mind. In fact, I have experienced that the opposite of this is also true. When the mind is peaceful, the diet is also healthy. For example, every time I ate junk food, my mind was agitated and I needed comfort, which I looked for in food. In fact, I still do this sometimes. Imagine how much harm mental stress can bring to the physical body! When work stress increases, out come the boxes of chocolates, the cold coffees, the pizzas, the burgers and the ice-creams. This, in turn, causes mood swings, leading to more stress and that leads to more junk food.

I had also been noticing that on the days when I ate spicy food, I felt particularly hot and found my heart rate to be slightly higher, causing me to be a bit on the edge with a little extra energy to expend. And on days when my processed sugar intake was high, I felt more inclined towards mood swings. Good thing that I noticed these things about my body and mind. Since fitness is always on the top of my list, when I was pregnant I thought it wise to visit a nutritionist who was trained and certified in understanding my food requirements in the best possible way. It was explained to me, and I paraphrase in lay terms, that when we eat any form of sugar (especially processed sugar) our energy levels shoot up only to dive down low as quickly, causing undefined mood swings, which lead to more cravings for sugar. That is one of the reasons why diet is crucial for mental health. This explains how processed sugar not only has physical effects, like obesity or gestational diabetes, on a pregnant woman but also has mental effects. To add to this revelation, I realized that I felt low when I was hungry and my energy levels were dropping. So, here's the vicious cycle that I found myself getting sucked into very often:

I would start my morning with positivity and fervour to

The Importance of Diet during Pregnancy

seize the day. I would eat healthy at that time. Somewhere in the middle, I would get stuck with work and feel hungry. I would ignore the hunger for a little while. My energy levels would start dropping and I would start feeling low. I would then need something to enhance my mood and start experiencing sugar cravings. I would get myself a cake and a cold coffee. I would then be in heaven. My sugar levels would rise and I would no longer be hungry, so I would skip the healthy meal I would have carried from home. But after a while, my sugar levels would come crashing down and I would crave more sugar. The healthy meal would by then have been wasted.

It became perfectly clear to me that a wholesome diet would take care of most of my concerns as a pregnant mother. A pregnant mother's health and wellness matter because their baby is safely tucked away inside them. So, naturally, I understood very early on in my pregnancy that the responsibility of feeling amazing and beautiful and all things positive is on me and not other people looking after me. As my mother often told me when I was a child, 'While you may decide your clothes depending on the fashion trends others create, the food you eat should only be for your benefit. So never eat to please anyone but yourself.' So, I started out targeting my physical fitness and eventually saw great results in every aspect of my day.

Before I delve into what exactly I ate while I was pregnant, I would like to bring to everybody's attention, once again, the fact that what you eat during pregnancy will define your post-partum health. You will continue to be on prescribed multi vitamins, etc., but your hormones will go through a drastic change immediately after the delivery. Your body will lose a lot of fluid, blood, along with a lot of nutrients, all of which will cause a sharp decline in your energy levels as well. Naturally, your health will also decline soon after the delivery and when the breastfeeding phase begins. The diet you consume during pregnancy will prove to be very helpful during this time, and trust me, you will need it as much then as you will need it while you are pregnant.

My day began with the juice of one gooseberry mixed in warm water. Gooseberries are extremely rich in Vitamin C, which is needed for good immunity and better absorption of iron in the body. But too much Vitamin C during pregnancy may pose a risk of preterm birth, and that is why I never risked overdoing the gooseberry juice. Another very tempting reason why I

The Importance of Diet during Pregnancy

still consume gooseberry juice every morning is that it strengthens hair. In fact, it must surely be because of the religious consumption of gooseberry juice during both my pregnancies that I did not experience the drastic hair loss most post-partum mothers complain about. In fact, my relationship with my hair underwent a huge change during my pregnancy, and there is no doubt in my mind that this was because of my fabulous diet.

As a child, my hair simply did not grow until I was about 13 or 14 years old. Everybody in my extended family made fun of me for having really scanty, thin, short hair. The more desperate I grew, the more fun they made; the more fun they made, the more desperate I grew. It was a vicious cycle. Then, miraculously, my hair started to grow when I entered my teens. Maybe it was the changing hormones. But even then, the longest my hair ever grew was a little below my shoulders, not long enough to be called waist length ever. And then I got pregnant. Suddenly, I started taking care of my diet, stopped eating all junk food, put my foot on the good health pedal in the engine of my life. And just like that, my hair started growing really fast and became extremely healthy and thick! Before my pregnancy was over, it was not just waist length, I could finally boast of hip-length hair! And the people who had made fun of my hair suddenly were in awe. That's the effect a good diet can have on your body and health. The pregnancy, for me, was just the beginning.

In the first trimester, I made sure I followed this up with one fruit, usually a fully ripe papaya or a banana. While we are on the topic of papayas, I must share my experience with this dreaded fruit during my first pregnancy. I love papayas but for the life of me I could not bring myself to touch the forbidden fruit because of so much misinformation in my brain. In numerous old Hindi films I had watched as a child, the vamp would feed raw papaya to the unsuspecting pregnant heroine in order to make her miscarry. Without a doubt, that trick always worked and resulted in a tear-laden damsel every single time! It took me three or maybe four visits to my gynaecologist at that time for her to convince me that eating ripe papaya in reasonable doses is actually good for my gut, which is under tremendous pressure anyway during pregnancy. She reassured me that only raw papayas pose a threat during pregnancy.

The papaya soon gave way to a fully loaded smoothie

The Importance of Diet during Pregnancy

when I found my appetite becoming quite voracious. I had grown to like my smoothies so much that I would go to bed dreaming about the smoothie I was going to have the next morning. I found myself waking up ravenous for that smoothie every day. I didn't know at that time that this smoothie would become an integral part of my diet for many years to come. To be precise, I continued to start my day with a smoothie way into my second postpartum journey, for roughly around eight long years! In fact, I have once again started having a smoothie off and on, especially when I feel that my calorie requirement has increased. Yes, that's how loyal I am to the things I love! The amazing things that I put in this magical smoothie are:

1 ripe banana
100 grams Greek yogurt (or any curd available at home)
1 teaspoon roasted flaxseeds
1 teaspoon roasted chia seeds
2 teaspoon organic unsweetened chocolate powder
2 seedless dates
3 tablespoon muesli with oats and nuts
1 tablespoon cold pressed coconut oil
8–10 dried goji berries (sometimes)

No wonder both my doctors were super happy with this concoction of mine. It literally kickstarted my day with so many nutrients and energy. And energy is something that a pregnant mother needs a lot of, no matter which stage she is in. This energy defines how her day goes and how efficient she feels, whether she feels like she is totally in control of things or whether she feels like she needs to sit down or take a nap. However, the first trimester is typically when no amount of food or rest makes a pregnant mother feel on top of things. This is the time when the blood volume increases to supply the developing placenta and foetal circulation. Hence, the heart pumps faster and stronger. The breathing is faster, the pulse is faster and the low iron absorption and rise in progesterone does not help either. Naturally then, this is the time when I started truly controlling the intake of processed sugar, because, let's face it, somebody like me who is always a go-getter did not need any more sudden dips in energy than I was already experiencing.

This brings me to the other popular notion I had been brought up with—sugar is, in fact, a necessity when you're pregnant. Well, it is, but not the processed kind. In fact, you need the sugar that the breaking down of food produces in your body naturally. The word 'sugar' causes confusion among many, and hence a lot of mothers feel that consuming processed sugar is imperative when pregnant. I have already explained why processed sugar is bad for me and particularly so when I was pregnant. Another reason to avoid it is the risk of addiction. An article published in 2017[1], which was just a year before I got pregnant the second time, stated that a study performed on rats proved that sugar was even more addictive than opioid drugs, like cocaine. Horrifying, is it not? The sugar mentioned in this case is the white, processed variety. But was this a fact anybody would believe? Obviously not, because, like me, they also have been brought up with the same notions about sugar. I was prepared to be attacked with many tempting laddoos and other sweets that I was sure would come my way from everybody who found out that I was pregnant. This was probably one of the most important reasons why I did not mind withholding the news of my pregnancy in the first trimester. If you decide to go the low processed sugar way, like me, you will realize that convincing somebody why you do not want to eat a treat

---

[1]'Is Sugar More Addictive than Cocaine', *New Hall Hospital*, 20 September 2017, https://tinyurl.com/3t5b5x5r. Accessed on 10 July 2023.

specially prepared for a pregnant mother just because it contains sugar is harder than you can imagine. The worst outcome of that is the judgement people pass sometimes in their heads and sometimes to your face, telling you to stop dieting while you are pregnant. So many people fail to understand that there is a difference in trying to be healthy and trying to be thin, and that quitting processed sugar is not about being thin but being healthy. I was to have my fair share of politely explaining this in the trimesters to follow. The constant reminder that right now, nothing is more important than my health for my own sake and my baby's, made everything else look easy.

While this raised many eyebrows in my case, the other thing that never went unnoticed was my consumption of soda. Here, I am talking about plain, unsweetened regular carbonated water. I really enjoyed the taste of the fizzy drink, and sometimes I had it with a squeeze of lemon and sometimes even with cold milk. I had to explain to a lot of people who told me to refrain from having sodas, that plain soda is just like sparkling water and the harmful variety of sodas are colas and aerated drinks, which are heavily loaded with sugar and caffeine. Besides, carbonated water also helps with nausea. In any case, moderation is

The Importance of Diet during Pregnancy

key when it comes to consuming anything when you are pregnant irrespective of whether it is good or bad for you.

Before I move on to other aspects of my diet that I was careful about when I was pregnant, I must touch upon morning sickness. Many mothers experience this in the first trimester. Thankfully, I was not one of them. But to think that the body is deprived of energy anyway, and then you end up puking what you ate almost each time, or at least feel like you would, is quite dreadful.

If you are one of those mothers, happier times are not far. The second trimester will be so much better; not only will the morning sickness subside but you will also see a sharp rise in the energy levels and the spring in your step will return. Additionally, that famous pregnancy glow and cute bump will start showing, inviting that envious attention which, let me warn you, is very addictive! But no matter which trimester you are in, energy requirements are going to be high always.

What I made sure of was that this energy came from the right sources. Hence, I focussed a lot on my protein intake. Protein is slow to be digested and, hence, provides energy for longer. My protein requirement was also high because I continued to go to the gym when I was pregnant. I ate breakfast post-workout every day. (Do not forget I used to have that banana and later that heavenly smoothie pre-workout.) I had two eggs daily along with one more portion of fruit and any form of carbohydrates, like oats, sooji upma, poha, moong dal chilla, besan chilla, dosa or different kinds of pancakes. I avoided bread as much as I could because that is just another kind of junk food. The protein that I consumed at lunch was the vegetarian kind. Pulses, lentils or paneer, and rice or roti for carbohydrates. The protein intake was also enhanced at dinner through either chicken, mutton or fish. I always made sure to eat home-cooked food, be it vegetarian or non-vegetarian. I ate food from restaurants only occasionally, during celebrations or when I travelled to Hong Kong in the second trimester of my second pregnancy.

This brings me to a topic regarding food that hugely concerns pregnant mothers. We've all heard how bad monosodium glutamate (MSG) is for pregnant mothers. This is something that is used generously in Chinese and Southeast Asian cooking. It is also found in some pre-made ready-to-eat sauces. How was I supposed to travel to Hong Kong then but not eat their delicious

The Importance of Diet during Pregnancy

cuisine? On one hand, my energy requirements were high and diet was of primary concern, and on the other, I was to watch the quantity of MSG that I consumed, meaning I had to watch the quantity of food I ate, since almost everything had MSG in it. A catch-22 situation, right? Well, if you are pregnant, you will find yourself in these situations more often than you would like to. To be honest, it did bother me a lot, but I was also sure that I wanted to visit a Southeast Asian destination for my vacation. So, once again, I ran to my gynaecologist with questions about whether MSG was alright for me to consume, and in what quantity, if at all. The answer I got was quite surprising. Pregnant Chinese women eat MSG as it is part of their staple diet. It is harmful only because of the high sodium content. Hence, if it is balanced with the amount of fluids consumed, it can be safe. This was such a relief to me because I love Chinese food. The golden rules I followed when eating Chinese were: first, I ordered things that had the maximum amount of greens in them and were as bland as could be—this ensured a low amount of MSG; secondly, I drank a lot of water, no matter how many times I had to visit the washroom. A complicated problem solved simply.

More than a Mama

Some of the other cravings that I experienced, besides cold coffee, were shallow-fried Bombay duck and jaggery-stuffed parantha. Many mothers are also weary of consuming sea food—how much of it is enough and what variety? I researched extensively on this subject. From what I found and what my gynaecologist advised, the cause for worry in seafood is the high mercury content, and there are certain seafoods that have more of it than others. Tuna, for example, is a forbidden fish, and so are crabs, lobsters and other shellfish. Much to my relief, Bombay duck is absolutely safe as long as it is consumed within reasonable quantities. I found myself gorging on home-cooked Bombay duck up to three times a week. Mohit would go to a nearby fish market and get loads of fresh bombil for me and Areeza, who also enjoys the delicacy. Mohit made friends with the ladies at the local fish market, and they always gave him the best of their inventory for the day. The market is right outside the main entrance of our society complex and is super convenient for us. Funnily enough, Mohit always tried to purchase from each one of them. Sometimes, he would buy Bombay duck from one and pomfret or some other fish from another on the same day. The lady he had not

The Importance of Diet during Pregnancy

purchased from on a particular day would take offense. The next time he would go to her, he would be greeted with a cold, '*Tu majhya karun kashala gheyto, tikdetch zaa, tee chya kadun ghey* (Why are you buying from me now? Go there and buy from her)?' Over the years, they have all grown to love Mohit and his visits, and Mohit, in turn, refrains from haggling too much with them. Even Areeza goes to the fish market with Mohit and the whole activity is a weekly bonding time for them. Due to this, we all have grown to include fresh fish in our weekly diet as well.

Consuming Bombay duck did wonders for my skin and hair during my pregnancy, and I thank my stars I had such a beneficial craving. The jaggery paranthas were not as low on calories as I would have liked, but the fact that jaggery is not half as bad as processed sugar was something that allowed me to binge every now and then, since weight gain was not my concern when I was pregnant. But I avoided overeating because jaggery can be a heat-inducing food and my cravings for it increased in the last few months, which were April and May, when temperatures in Mumbai soar. An interesting thing to note is that the last trimester is when a pregnant mother gains the maximum amount of weight and, if you have been good throughout, now is not the time to give in to temptation when you're right at the finish line. The weight gain at this point should be for the right reasons and the most important reason is that the baby is also putting on fat in this trimester. The reason for a mother's weight gain should definitely not be because of overeating or over-consumption of junk food.

During pregnancy, one of the most difficult things to deal with were the midnight hunger pangs. *Here I am, trying to eat healthy, and yet ruining it all by gaining empty calories when my body's metabolism is at the slowest.* If any of you have had that same thought then let me nip it in the bud. Pregnancy is not a time to count calories. You will, in all probability, end up consuming almost double the amount of calories you require when you're not pregnant, but trust me, your body needs it. Pregnant women can see a fluctuation in their blood pressure as well as blood sugar levels if they do not pay attention to their diet. The only thing that you must try to do is eat something that will add value to your diet rather than just empty calories. The food choices I kept handy for midnight hunger pangs were nuts and dry fruits, like

The Importance of Diet during Pregnancy

almonds, figs, walnuts, cashews and dates, a spoonful of muesli mixed with curd or grated and cooked carrots with a dash of jaggery. Sometimes, I reheated and ate just the leftover vegetable that had been cooked for dinner the previous night.

Let me move on to some of the other things I was particular about during my pregnancy. Coconut water deserves a special mention. Coconut water was my daily mid-morning meal. I had a scheduled coconut water delivery in office every day at around 12.00 p.m. and always made sure to have it as soon as it arrived. Anything natural does not have a very long shelf life and coconut water stays fresh for as long as 24 hours, after which you cannot be sure of its taste and freshness any longer. It should be consumed within 10 minutes of cracking it open, just like any fruit should be consumed freshly cut. All these things were easy to follow, and I followed them diligently.

Apart from this, there was a long list of things that I consumed, by increasing their intake in my diet. Green leafy vegetables were part of my daily diet, sometimes cooked in Indian style and sometimes just boiled with a dash of garlic or some other herb. Palak, methi, bok choy, mooli bhaji, khatti bhaji, sarson and even fresh coriander leaves are a few leafy vegetables that are commonly available. I also ate simple salads with cucumber, spring onion and tomatoes. I tried my best to eat at regular intervals and eat extra when I felt hungry even though it may not have been time to eat yet. Basically, I was trying, once again, to connect with my body on a much deeper level, where lunch may be early or late but was in sync with my body's requirements.

A pregnancy diet should be carefully discussed with your healthcare provider. But whatever you choose, remember that this diet is going to impact your post-partum years as well. This in no way means that you need to chart out a healthy meal plan for yourself, but just that it helps to be mindful. Your energy levels (and you will need a high dose of these once the baby arrives) matter. There is bound to be imbalance in your mental well-being too, every now and then, and a good diet will go a long way in managing it. Most importantly, the ability to control your body and mind the way you want to depends on the diet you consume during your pregnancy. When I was pregnant, my mother always told me that the pregnancy years define all my future years and, hence, should never

The Importance of Diet during Pregnancy

be taken lightly. So, while pregnancy cravings may be many, remember to be mindful while eating anything. I took this time to correct all my bad eating habits and form good ones. If all this is overwhelming, just refer to these pointers and let your body decide for you what and when to eat:

- Eat when you're hungry.
- Eat well without any apprehension.
- Remember you are eating this for yourself and not for two as many believe.
- Before eating sugar or any junk food, remember the ill-effects it can have on you and your baby. If you still feel like consuming it, go ahead.
- Never let guilt over come you if you do end up eating something you shouldn't. Guilt will harm you more than the junk food ever will.
- Last but not the least, your happiness is of utmost importance always. So, if eating a small amount of something that may be a bit unhealthy will give you happiness, go ahead and do it, Mama!

Now that you have read everything about my pregnancy days and how I managed my health and fitness, let me tell you how I managed to return to my pre-pregnancy diet and fitness (read sanity) once my baby was in my arms.

5

Post-partum Fitness: Slow and Steady Wins the Race

In my childhood, I was always a waif-thin girl, laughed at by fellow students and made to feel conscious about my weight or rather the lack of it. I remember asking my Nanaji, who was a passionate homeopath and a magnetotherapist, to give me some magical pill that would make me put on weight. To this, he would laugh and say to me, '*Jab tu badi ho jayegi toh mujhse bolegi ki nanaji, mujhe patle hone ki dawai de do* (When you grow up, you will ask me for a magical pill to lose weight)!'

I never understood the logic behind this and would feel helpless while convincing him to give me that secret pill. Little did I know then that neither is there a magic pill to put on weight nor is there one to lose it.

But before we delve into my weight loss and fitness journey, I would like to mention that the biggest struggle for any new mother is not to lose weight but to learn to love her body just the way it is. All mothers are beautiful, and all mothers are victorious warriors. You have already climbed the toughest mountain when you became a mother after carrying your baby for nine months inside your womb and bringing it out in the world with a smile on your face. This was all with the help of this beautiful and strong body that you possess. Unfortunately, nobody told me this when I saw my own body in a negative light, expecting it to endure even more than it already had.

My first tryst with weight gain was when I delivered my first baby. No, I had not put on substantial weight during the pregnancy. My arms looked skinny, my face looked the same, I even fit into most of my pre-pregnancy clothes barring the ones that were tight around my abdomen. I gained 10 kg during my first pregnancy and, from my calculations, I thought—since the amniotic fluid weighs

Post-partum Fitness: Slow and Steady Wins the Race

more or less the same as the baby, after I delivered my baby, who was 2.5 kg—I would be straight 5 kg down on the scale. I was in for a rude shock because when I came back home after three days—I was still 10 kg up, even when there was no baby in my tummy, no amniotic fluid, my arms suddenly looked dimpled, my thighs looked rounder, and I still looked five months pregnant! How was I going to lose this weight? Because my expectations had been so unreasonable, the outcome naturally threw me into a state of panic.

It can be pretty daunting if you put on this much weight. I remembered my Nanaji's words and missed him so much. If only he were alive, I could call him and tell him how true his words had been. (And if he did have that magic pill to lose weight, I'd have asked him to give it to me without wasting another minute!) The realization that I neither had my Nanaji nor a magic pill made my stomach turn. I felt the frustration that so many mothers the world over must be feeling. The fact that I had not even begun to understand the meaning of being a mother only made things worse because all I could think of was that I wanted to lose weight! How was I supposed to enjoy my motherhood? How shallow this kind of thinking was, and how brutally I treated my own self is something I learnt when I set off on a desperate mission to be thin again. The biggest problem was that I was trying to be thin, not fit. It is fitness that is of utmost importance once you become a mother, considering the amount of running around physically, and the amount of patience you require in the years to come. There was so much I was about to learn in the months to come.

The only thing in my favour at that time was the fact that I had delivered naturally, and not via surgery. In hindsight, what if it was not in fact a positive thing? It is because I had had a normal delivery that I thought I did not need as much rest as a C-section mother does. I was barely 30 days into my first post-partum recovery when I started skipping again, much to my mother's horror! She begged me to stop skipping, even if I couldn't refrain from doing some other kind of activity to lose weight. She tried so hard to make me believe that weight loss was not going to be an issue, but my health could be if I was not careful at this point. She couldn't have been more right! A week into skipping, I had an episode of incontinence; I involuntarily peed while skipping, and then was left wondering how I became so wet. When

Post-partum Fitness: Slow and Steady Wins the Race

you have a baby, all the muscles around your core are sensitive. While you're pregnant, your bladder cannot take the slightest of pressure and you need to pee ever so often to keep it comfortable. Naturally, the muscles that help you with controlling your excretion need to get their strength back because they have also been through so much.

For all mothers who might feel as desperate as I once did, look into the mirror and see how beautiful you are. Today, I realize what immense power lay within me and how I was wasting it trying to achieve unimportant things. However, the positive takeaway from this incident was that this was the exact time when I decided to take charge of my fitness goals in a healthy way. I remembered how I had taken my body for granted through my growing up years, eating the wrong kind of food, never understanding the importance of physical activity, and always getting away with all this without any trouble. But I was in my thirties now, a baby mama, and it was time to grow up.

I started going to the gym in my society. I focussed on improving my energy levels, better haemoglobin, better hair health, better skin and better efficiency in my everyday chores. I was happier and calmer and was able to spend quality time with Areeza. The weight training that I learnt during this time also helped me form the enviable mind–body connection that I have. Everyone has their fair share of experiences and learnings that define their epiphanous moments. For me, it was the incontinence. Such incidents have made me feel that what had happened was not fair, or I deserved better, but they have also invariably made me grow as a person and made me who I am today. This incident, for example, was the catalyst for me to begin my fitness journey and along with it, being able to enjoy my first motherhood journey with little Areeza. I started to learn everything step by step.

Hence, after my second pregnancy, I had a very different experience. By then, I knew that losing weight was secondary to being healthy and fit. I also knew that my responsibilities would double since I was now to take care of two children while also running two companies with Mohit. I knew that my real power lay in my mind and that that was the organ I should work on developing the most.

I opted for hypnobirthing the second time. For those of you who are unacquainted with what that is, it is a birthing method that focusses on relaxation. The

Post-partum Fitness: Slow and Steady Wins the Race

techniques involve meditative pain management and zero medical interference unless absolutely necessary. Usually, in hypnobirthing, the most important person in the room with the mother is the husband or the birthing partner, who could be a doula or a midwife, and a doctor is called in if there is an emergency; medical help is needed. I started working on the power of the mind from the beginning of the pregnancy and meditation helped me go through the initial 9–10-hour-long labour without any trouble; I sat down on my chair while Mohit made sure nobody interrupted me. We had already shared a copy of our birth plan with the entire hospital staff and had got their approval.

Naturally then, I was not prepared for the emergency C-section I was taken in for after I was 8-cm dilated. I had never imagined in my wildest dreams that I would be a C-section mother after having such a healthy and smooth pregnancy. Hence, my knowledge or experience about a C-section post-partum recovery was zilch. I began to doubt being able to ever come back to my pre-pregnancy fitness levels.

This could have led to desperation rearing its ugly head once again, but I was more equipped to handle the pressure this time. I was already trying to make my peace with the fact that I would probably never work out the way I used to—going up to 3,000 skips a day, running 5 km at a stretch, lifting weights with ease and running around swiftly while getting on with my everyday chores, among other things. But the strength that I now possessed as a mother kept nagging me to not give up. I called up all my friends and other mothers who had delivered via C-section, I googled celebrities who had delivered via C-section, in the hope that there will be one, just one, mother who would tell me that undergoing a C-section did not change her lifestyle. All my efforts were in vain. However, I found the strength within me to become that person who can inspire somebody like me and break the myth that C-section deliveries meant getting back to pre-pregnancy fitness level is impossible or harder.

Good news, dear mothers! It it is absolutely possible to achieve all your fitness goals and more even after a C-section delivery, if you take one step at a time, allowing your body to heal. It was after the C-section delivery that I learnt to do push ups, pulls ups and chin ups, something I always thought only men could do. I can lift double the amount of weight I could lift prior to my second pregnancy, my stamina has increased in the gym, and the toned arms and flat tummy are just a bonus! The only mantra I used was 'go slow'.

What to Expect Immediately After the Delivery

The initial few days after my C-section were really hard for me. I had severe side effects from the spinal tap. I had a massive migraine when I sat down, which became milder when I lay down. This lasted for the first few days, accompanied by a partial loss of hearing in one of my ears. Phew! As daunting as all this sounds, it only lasted for two or three days and is also uncommon. Different mothers may experience different things, but the only uncomfortable thing that every post-partum mother faces is the breast engorgement and the struggle with the let-down. If you are prepared for this, you find that this phase keeps getting substantially better each day. If you have a choice and the means, you must take help from a lactation consultant; it really did help me. Like a lot of second-time mothers, I initially thought that I knew what I was doing and that I didn't need any help with breastfeeding. However, Arham's way of latching on was very different from that of Areeza's, and I ended up with extremely painful, bleeding nipples that made a perfectly simple task rough and difficult. I called the lactation consultant much later and her help proved to be beneficial.

Coming back to the recovery: if you have had a natural birth, you will recover miraculously fast. A natural birth is one where no external or medical interference is needed and the whole birthing process happens naturally. If you have had a normal delivery, you may have stitches in the perineum that will take a few weeks to heal. From my experience of my first delivery, which was a normal one, these stitches are uncomfortable but not painful, and once they heal, life goes back to absolute normal. Needless to say, every experience can be different.

If you have had a C-section, like I did the second time, you will feel a lot of pain and discomfort near the stitches. I had trouble sitting up and lying down and had to use a catheter for a good two days after the surgery. This, I might add, was my choice, since I was asked to remove it after 24 hours but decided to keep it for a little longer (since getting up felt impossible). This was

Post-partum Fitness: Slow and Steady Wins the Race

not a very good decision, and I would advise you to push yourself as per your physiotherapist's advice and try to walk to the washroom when needed. I was not strong enough to take my physiotherapist's advice and stand up, and I think this had more to do with my mental strength at the time rather than physical. The healing will be a lot faster if you can just start sitting, standing and lying down by yourself. All these things might sound tough, but the good news is, by day three or four, your doctor will ask you to go home, and trust me, by then you will already have improved 30 per cent!

The remaining 70 per cent recovery should usually take three months. Even if you feel like you are ready and healed, you must wait for three months before beginning your fitness journey. Yup, I know, you may be eager. I know I was, but I vehemently insist on this since starting too soon will only make your fitness journey slow, tedious and frustrating. For the first one month, I just gave myself time to settle in. Breastfeeding took up most of my time because I was struggling to breastfeed exclusively for as long as I could, trying to find the most comfortable positions and corners of the house. I must add that given the planner that I am (read: Virgo), I had a breastfeeding corner designed in Arham's room where I had everything that I needed while feeding him. I designed the couch and had it custom-made; there were armrests at the perfect distance, cushions for my back to be rested, a side table to put my paraphernalia, like wet wipes, muslin cloths, burp cloths, diapers. etc. But once Arham arrived, I realized that the couch I had so carefully designed was really uncomfortable! And like most mothers, I found myself plonked in my own room on my own bed using my own pillow to breastfeed him.

The reason I had gone to these lengths to design these things prior to the baby's arrival had been because of my experience with Areeza. Since I had no experience when she was born, I had collected all these things after she was born. I realized the market is flooded with things to support a breastfeeding mother! And a feeding pillow is something that I used to swear by and wonder why other mothers sit in such uncomfortable positions to feed their babies, ending up with backaches. But sure enough, my own experiences turned out to be useless when it came to breastfeeding little Arham. As time goes by, you too will find your own special place and position to breastfeed your baby.

Post-partum Fitness: Slow and Steady Wins the Race

By the time I developed a breastfeeding relationship with Arham, I was walking around the house and taking charge of most of the domestic responsibilities. Although I had help with the cooking and cleaning, I was really struggling to find a good nanny for little Arham who could just watch him while he slept, so I could at least start taking a walk. This was good in a way. I was still not ready to step out for a walk because then there would have been no way of keeping track of how much I had walked. I wanted to keep track, not to see how I could up my performance, but rather to ensure I didn't overdo it. So, I started taking walks inside the house, 10 minutes a day, even if I felt like I could walk more. I am somebody who is used to pushing the envelope and, hence, constantly reminded myself to do less because, at that time, less is more. I gradually increased the 10 minutes to 45 minutes a day, after which I was ready to take my walks down to the garden.

After around two months of these walks, the rounds within the little space were becoming too many to even count anymore! I was walking from my bedroom door through the hall and passage up to my neighbour's front door. These walks will always be memorable since every time I passed by the big rocking chair in my hall where I put Arham down for a nap during that time, I would look at his adorable little body and tiny little face and smile every single time. I would play soft music, so he would not be disturbed and the music would serve as white noise for him. When I would get bored of walking in the same small area, I would chant *Nam Myoho Renge Kyo* and try to make music in my mind matching this with the rhythm of my feet! Although I am not a Buddhist, I sometimes chant this, and it calms me down.

The Post-Partum Fitness Journey Begins

Right after the three months were over, I went to my OB-GYN and he did a thorough check-up. He palpated the sutures and told me that they had healed beautifully, but the abdominal muscles were completely lax and care should be given while resuming workouts. He advised me to go slow and stop a certain exercise if it made me uncomfortable or caused pain. In other words, he reiterated my own mantra to me: 'Listen to your body'. I was going to do that anyway.

The first day I went to the gym, I felt really awkward.

Post-partum Fitness: Slow and Steady Wins the Race

I could not fit into my regular sportswear and was still wearing my pregnancy sportswear. I was wary of lifting a dumbbell for fear of not being able to complete a set. I had never felt so much fear at the gym ever before. In fact, the gym had always been my happy place. Before heading to the gym, I was reminded of the very first time I ever went for a screen test.

That day changed my life; in fact, it defined it. I was 19 years old and had got a call from a TV producer to come and audition for an anchoring job. How terrified I was, thinking about the lines I would have to speak in front of a camera! I rejected the thought in my head. At that point, my mother came to me and told me, 'Chhavi, go and audition. What is the worst that could happen? You will make a fool of yourself, na? Go make a fool of yourself and come back.' I went there, 'made a fool of myself' and landed the project only to go on to become one of the best TV anchors Delhi had seen during that time.

Once again, at the age of 38, I told myself, 'Chhavi, go to the gym and make a fool of yourself. That is the worst you can do anyway.' With this thought, I went to the gym and each day, I came back not just not having made a fool of myself, but increasing my stamina and competency a little. My growth in the gym was reasonably fast, since my muscle memory kicked in as soon as I started lifting weights. If you have never been to a gym, your progress may be slower, since you need to develop your muscle memory, but there will be progress for sure, which you will notice each day. Do not be afraid to 'make a fool of yourself'.

I want to take a moment here to thank my mom. Teaching me how to make a fool of myself was one of the most important life lessons she has taught me.

In the first one month of going to the gym, I only lifted light weights and concentrated on the number of repetitions rather than the weight itself. For example, if I had been lifting a 7.5 kg dumbbell for bicep curls before my pregnancy, I started with 3.5 kg, but did 15–20 repetitions instead of 10 or 12. This helped me slowly get used to the form. As I mentioned previously, the form of each exercise is extremely important since bad form will not only hamper you from seeing the benefits but also put you at risk of injury. If you wish to start weight training but have no previous experience, a good idea is to let a trainer guide you initially till you start understanding your own comfort level. I did the same the first time

Post-partum Fitness: Slow and Steady Wins the Race

around. Weight training cannot be started afresh while you're pregnant but is definitely a great option if you are looking at post-partum weight loss in the right way. Remember to never let anybody push you into doing anything your body does not feel comfortable with, since, as a post-partum mother, only you know your limits. That is the reason I discontinued using a personal trainer after learning what I needed to know about working out in a gym. I believe that I know my limits well and know how much to push. Nobody else can know how my body feels at a given time while performing a certain exercise. I can either feel the burn, not feel it at all, feel it a little extra or feel the need to feel it a bit more. Whatever it may be, if I decide my limits, I am the safest. These limits feel different on different days because your fatigue level, the food you ate the previous day, how you slept, etc. will play an important role. My limits may be different from yours. I feel great in terms of my fitness and energy levels, but there are still many exercises I cannot go ahead with. However, I never aim to compete with somebody who is doing better. When it comes to fitness, you are your only competition. Build from where you are and keep taking it higher. And, if you feel uncomfortable taking charge of your fitness and wish to hire a professional trainer or take guidance the way I did when I started out, my advice to you would be to stay away from online/offline weight loss programmes that are not customized for you. Even if they are designed for post-partum mothers, I would recommend a programme that caters to your requirements.

I did 10 minutes of cardio every day, no matter the body part I targeted. This was either running at a slow speed of 8–8.5 or getting on the cross trainer or elliptical. Not much different from when I was pregnant, right? I also added a day of swimming each week. My swimming was as intense as it was during pregnancy which, as I mentioned, was 45–50 minutes non-stop, alternating between strokes. I never really saw the point of increasing the duration to more than this. I also started doing planks very regularly at this time. I could not hold a plank for too long, but simply started with my own comfort point, which was roughly 20 seconds. I remembered to not hold my stomach too tight, but merely worked on rebuilding the abdominal muscles. I never forgot that the idea to come to the gym was not to look thin but to be strong.

It took me roughly three months to resume my full-fledged routine and lift the same amount of weight I

Post-partum Fitness: Slow and Steady Wins the Race

used to lift before I was pregnant. I looked great and felt even better. My body weight was still not the same as the pre-pregnancy weight because I had not been able to make the necessary diet adjustments yet, but I was loving the way I was looking! This was also the time I wore my pre-pregnancy jeans for the first time and it felt great—not because I had lost weight but because a pair of worn-in jeans just feels so comfortable!

I often talk about comfort because it becomes one of the most important things as you grow up, post-partum or not. Everything needs to be comfortable. Your clothes, your jeans, the shoes you wear, the chair you sit in, the bed you sleep in, even the friends you hang out with have to make you feel comfortable. And it is comfort that helps you in your fitness journey as well. It tells you what your limits are and how much of those limits you are ready to push.

For all the mothers who have never trained with weights before, I would like to tell you that you will never have an injury if you work inside your comfort zone. However, you will not see results if you don't come out of the comfort zone! Does that sound too confusing? It's important to define 'comfort' and 'comfort zone' first.

Any kind of weightlifting has to be measured by its own parameters. For example, just because you are capable of lifting a bucket filled with water from the floor, it doesn't necessarily mean you can also lift the same bucket if it's kept on the top shelf. Correct? In fact, even if you are capable of lifting the bucket from the floor, you may not be able to lift it without arching your back, bending your knees or bending your elbows. Correct? In this case, lifting the bucket from the floor is within your 'comfort zone' but can cause an injury if you don't feel 'comfortable' while doing it. You do this by coming into the correct position of an arched back or bent knees. This is called 'form' in weight training. You will never go wrong if the correct form is adhered to. But to increase your stamina, you will have to get out of your comfort zone at some point and try to lift the bucket kept on the top shelf. But even while doing so, if you feel uncomfortable, you are in for trouble. That is why, when you are weight training, you might lift heavier in a certain exercise and lighter in the other, till you stretch your weightlifting capacity by maintaining comfort (form) but getting out of your comfort zone (increasing weight/repetition).

I apply this formula every time I feel like I'm getting

Post-partum Fitness: Slow and Steady Wins the Race

into a comfort zone with my training. There is no standard exercise pattern that I can tell you other than these small but important basics about pushing your limits to see the best results while ensuring an injury-free journey. Increase the weight every seven days, or increase the repetitions, or increase the holding time or the negative time while performing an exercise, or swap the exercise with another one that feels new to the body and the muscles, or simply give yourself a change of scenery. If you apply these principles, you will be able to design a workout that suits you the best.

Around seven months post-partum, I started feeling the need to up my performance level by introducing something challenging. I wanted to start skipping again since skipping, in my opinion, is the single most effective exercise to see instant results on core strengthening. But after the C-section, I was petrified to even try this. I took advice from my OB-GYN. He told me that there was no harm in trying, since I had healed completely, and merely reminded me to listen to my body. I might add that he too was blown away, like most people, when I told him I used to go up to 3,000 skips at a time. But let me remind you this is my benchmark. So, when I started skipping again, I decided to start with 100 a day, but went up to 300 the first day itself because I needed to start building up from my own capacity. There is no competition, there is no judgement. For you that number may be 10, if you ever want to go down that road. I have male friends who cannot go beyond 500 a day and that is perfect for them. There are others, like my husband, who never even learnt how to skip and are perfectly fine resorting to other means like cycling or a high-impact sport. I always say, choose your poison and then train your body to get used to it. That is the ultimate high. For me, it is running, swimming, skipping and weight training. For you, it may be yoga, pilates, Zumba, or any other form of exercise; what is important is that you always challenge yourself to perform just a little better than you did yesterday, and you will see results.

Most Frequently Asked Question: How Did I Lose the Belly?

Let me begin by saying that just like there are no shortcuts, there is no way of spot reduction too, and there are definitely no guarantees that just because it worked for

Post-partum Fitness: Slow and Steady Wins the Race

me, it will work for you. A flat tummy is a by-product of discipline—the discipline of waking up early, eating right, not giving in to idle temptations all the time, working out very regularly, understanding what gets you the results that you are looking for and what does not, and (as unrelated as it may sound) ridding your body of toxins as much as you can. Are you ready to put in that kind of commitment? I have had so many mothers telling me that all they want is to lose the belly fat, but how can I tell them that they will either lose all the weight or none at all? You will be amazed that the things I have already mentioned will get you to lose that stubborn belly fat too, as much as it will tone your arms and legs and butt and back. Almost all leg exercises work on the lower stomach muscles too, and many of the exercises that require you to lift weight also require you to hold your core muscles extra tight in order to get the strength to lift, thereby working on your core too. There are some abdomen-specific exercises that I perform at least times a week. But even three years after the C-section, I still feel tightness in the lower abdomen muscles and hence I don't overdo anything related to that area. Too much working out on the stomach area can cause a lot of other complications that you seriously don't need. So, I would suggest that you just focus on your overall fitness and learn to love the stomach you get in return. The only exercise that I find harmless is performing different kinds of planks.

Before you start out on the journey to achieving whatever fitness-related goals you set for yourself, remember that you are beautiful. Even after doing so much, there are days when I feel bloated. It could be hormonal, or something I ate the day before, or an upset stomach or water retention, but as long as I feel active and energetic, I simply choose to wear a loose pair of jeans and forget about it because I know tomorrow will be a new day and a new story. My body supported me when I needed it to nurse a new life, and now it's my turn to support it when it's losing its youth and elasticity, isn't it?

But fitness is nothing if it's not combined with a proper diet. If you feel you're following the same diet you were before you got pregnant but it's not agreeing with your body anymore, it's because the post-partum diet needs to be far more disciplined than the pre-pregnancy diet. Let me share mine with you.

6

Being Healthy: Post-partum Diet

Diet. I understood the true meaning of this word when I became a mother. I believe that is the way it happens with most mothers. If not their own diet, they do bring the roof down worrying about their little one's diet. Is she drinking enough milk? Is she eating enough? Is she getting the nutrition she needs? Is there enough calcium, enough iron, minerals, fibre, enough everything in her diet? And every time something goes wrong or does not go according to how we imagine, like the little one not pooping at the regular time, pooping a different colour, not eating during meal times, not sleeping enough, crying too much, or any such thing, the first thing we wonder as mothers is if we gave her something wrong to eat. We might even wonder if we should be refraining from giving her a particular thing to eat which might be causing this discomfort. While thinking of our baby's dietary needs as something that strengthens her, we apply a completely different standard to our own diets as mothers. We now start looking at our diet as a means to lose weight. In fact, I have seen many mothers who feel that the diet they consume should be reduced substantially to feel healthy and light. Many mothers even borderline starve themselves.

The reasons for these drastic measures are not hard to understand. Since many of us put on a reasonable amount of weight during pregnancy, we feel a little helpless when it comes to finding ways to lose this weight. When pregnant, the weight looks appealing to us and everybody around us. We feel comfortable in loose clothing and get used to being admired by everyone and being told confidence-boosting things like how cute we look, how much we glow, etc. Naturally, after we deliver, these compliments go towards the little one and although the love we feel towards the new arrival is strong, sometimes

Being Healthy: Post-partum Diet

without realizing it, we do start feeling neglected. We look in the mirror and feel like we liked our pregnant selves better. The glow goes away, the hormones being all over the place does not flatter us, the hair fall begins, and the weight does not look cute anymore. Since our physical health is not at its prime because we are busy healing and recovering from the delivery, we neglect our fitness to the point of no return, and then we feel it's too late to start losing the post-partum weight. And once we feel like we are ready to begin, for the lack of better understanding, we take out all our frustration on the food we eat, constantly cutting down on the quantity, and thereby the essential nutrients.

My question to all mothers is this: When we understand the importance of nutrients in our children's lives, why do we fail to see it in our own? When our own health is under scrutiny, we list the things that we should stop consuming rather than the list of things that we should start or continue to consume to be healthy. Losing weight does not mean cutting down on calories; it simply means cutting down on unnecessary calories and increasing the ones that your body needs in abundance, thereby maintaining a balance. You can lose weight in a healthy way with a careful diet plan while increasing your energy and fitness levels. But, like I said, this diet needs a lot of discipline.

My post-partum diet was a lot more disciplined after the second pregnancy than the first one. I made these changes for a couple of reasons. In my first post-partum journey, I was younger. I was all of 31. The hormones were far more in control at that age, metabolism was much faster and the body was much more used to digesting different kinds of food without having long-term effects. If you are a young mother, you definitely have an advantage. Also, I had undergone a normal delivery, which made a lot of difference. The biggest difference was the amount of weight I needed to manage. I had gained 10 kg in the first pregnancy as opposed to the 17 kg I gained during the second. The second time, my mother could only stay with me for 15 days, out of which a good seven passed in anticipation of the new arrival, since Arham took his own sweet time to come into the world. I did not have an elder family member staying with me and I had to get on my feet sooner than I had wished to.

We all know that the post-partum diet is extremely important to regain the strength the body has lost and

Being Healthy: Post-partum Diet

to assist in breastfeeding. Hence, a lot of well-meaning mothers and mothers-in-law advise you to have gond ke laddoos and methi laddoos and other breastmilk-enhancing foods. To begin with, nobody did all that for me. And to top it all, while I was all for the gond and the methi, I was not at all in favour of consuming the unnecessary, not to mention, absolutely useless processed sugar these things contain. So, I searched and searched for something that had the goodness sans the other ingredients. For a long time, I didn't find anything and, hence, went to the kitchen myself to prepare my own not-so-tasty concoction of *panjeeri* which had ragi instead of wheat and jaggery instead of sugar. If I am honest, it turned out so bad that I could not bear the thought of consuming it daily, that too multiple times a day. Now, in retrospect, considering I'm in the YouTube business, how did I not think to check for a recipe on YouTube? I'm pretty sure I would've found one and I would advise you to do the same, even if you have somebody cooking it for you, rather than consuming empty calories in the form of white sugar. Eventually, though, my darling husband found these yummy laddoos online that were up to my standards of taste and health! I might have devoured them a bit too much for them to stop me from gaining an extra kilogram or two though. However, I wasn't worried because this time I was clear that post-partum recovery time is not the time to worry about piling on weight. Everybody piles on a little bit of weight post-partum because it is the body's mechanism to protect itself from the after-effects of what it has just been through. Even for breastfeeding, you need a little bit of fat around your body. This weight, however, is not always the weight you gained during pregnancy but also the weight you gain post-partum. There's a lot of different research I read at the time and, to be honest, it was quite baffling. The only thing important is to just eat healthy things, without obsessing too much about it. So, I decided to follow a particular diet for the first three months when I was focussing only on the body's healing and then altered it to match my body's requirement once I resumed working out.

Diet During The First Three Months Post-partum

While my mother was staying with me, she forced me to drink a healthy concoction. She would boil some jeera and saunf in three litres of water and ask me to drink

Being Healthy: Post-partum Diet

only that whenever I felt thirsty. Although she told me that I should not be drinking plain water at all for the first six weeks or so, I continued to drink at least two extra bottles of plain water over and above the three litres that she prepared for me. Even after she left for Delhi, she gave me strict instructions to have this every day for as many days as I could, and I followed this instruction for a whole month or so. I cannot tell you what benefits this has for a lactating mother. Instead, I suggest you ask your own mother or mother-in-law! The other piece of my mother's advice that I tried my best to follow was to completely avoid cold things. She said to refrain from drinking my preferred beverage, cold coffee and that, I think, was the biggest sacrifice I may have made as a mother. Okay, that was an exaggeration, but it surely felt like that at the time, since every little thing seemed to tick me off, and on a scale of one to ten, I was emotionally charged at eleven within a few seconds. And just knowing that the hormones are playing havoc with my mind didn't seem to help much.

There was also a lot of information that I received from fellow mothers and older (read: wiser) mothers. I did not, however, find any logic in most of their advice, even though I sincerely tried to consider every piece of advice I received. 'You need to eat a *lot!*' was something I heard a *lot!* To be honest, this sounded more like a threat than advice. A breastfeeding mother needs to consume 450–500 calories more than her daily calorific requirement prior to being pregnant. My daily calorific requirement was 1,800–1,900, which meant that I needed to up it to just 2,350 calories per day. Around 500 of these were instantly received from my morning smoothie. Not that I have ever counted how many calories a particular food has, but this did give me a fairly decent idea that I needed to consume roughly 25 per cent additional calories in a day. In the first three months, these calories were divided through the day and the night and there were hardly any periods of time when I was not eating. I ate as and when I felt hungry, I ate every time I breastfed, I ate during night feeds, I ate as soon as I woke up, I ate in my free time, and I ate any other time I may have forgotten to mention! But the trick was to always eat small portions of the healthiest things, which nourished my body as a whole and helped me produce nutritious milk for my baby. I ate salads, milk, curd, fruits, vegetables, grains, pulses, chicken, fish, mutton, eggs, seeds, nuts, butter, ghee, oils and more. I did not eat sugar, pizzas, burgers, deep-fried foods, savouries, etc. I began to lose weight by just eating right and continuing to breastfeed.

There are also multiple theories around whether certain vegetables are gassy for the baby. I would just like to take this opportunity to inform my readers that babies' digestive tracts develop after they are born. Naturally, then, you witness a lot of gassy and colicky cries for the first three months. This in no way means that the baby is unable to consume certain foods because once they have been processed through the mother's body and fed to the baby as the mother's milk, they are, in most cases, safe for the baby. Of course, this cannot be applied to babies who have a food allergy or sensitivity.[2] I ate all notorious foods, like rajma, potatoes, chana, bhindi, etc., because I believed that even if the food is causing difficulty, I wanted my baby's digestive system to be so solid that nothing ever gives him any trouble in his future years, which pretty much means all his life. Like most babies, Arham also stopped getting colicky at three months.

I also continued to consume caffeine moderately and

---

[2] '5 Breastfeeding Diet Myths', *Johns Hopkins Medicine*, https://tinyurl.com/4p9ape2n. Accessed on 6 July 2023.

sometimes even had a glass of cold coffee against my mother's wishes. However, I made sure to allow it to come closer to room temperature rather than having it absolutely chilled. I did not worry at all about specific meal times; I pretty much felt hungry every time I fed little Arham and hence fed myself each time, irrespective of what time of the day or night it was.

Diet after Three Months Post-partum

There is no visible result if a workout does not have an accompanying healthy diet. I did not go to a nutritionist at this point because I felt I was fairly aware of my body's needs when I began my workouts. Besides, I did not want to get too particular and fussy about what I ate and wanted to keep it a little flexible to maintain my sanity, which was really important for me at this point and should be for every mother.

Keeping these things in mind, the first thing that I eliminated from my diet was any form of sweets. As it turns out, blood sugar and insulin levels fluctuate, not just due to processed sugar but any form of sugar that gives the body an overdose of carbohydrates.[3] This makes perfect sense and I thought to myself: now that I am going to be working harder than ever, I do not want my body to have blood sugar lows caused by insulin irregularities. This meant no jaggery, no honey, no stevia, no artificial sweetener, no erythritol or any other sugar substitute. Having said that, I did continue having fruits and dried fruits because I am all for natural sugars and no amount of weight gain can stop me from consuming them. This is simply because I always prioritize the nutritional value of any food item over its calorie quotient. According to research, fructose is not only harmless but also helpful. For example, berries can actually blunt the insulin spike from high-glycaemic foods, like white bread. This is because the fibre in fruits acts like a protective gel in the stomach and small intestine that slows the release of sugar. Also, certain phytonutrients in fruits appear to block the absorption of sugar through the gut wall into the bloodstream.[4] The antioxidants in fruits also do a lot

---

[3]Mathur, Kushagra, et al., 'Effect of Artificial Sweeteners on Insulin Resistance Among Type-2 Diabetes Mellitus Patients', *Journal of Family Medicine and Primary Care*, Vol. 9, No. 1, 2020, pp. 69–71, https://tinyurl.com/4ty52w4b. Accessed on 6 July 2023.

[4]Calvano, Aron, et al., 'Dietary Berries, Insulin Resistance and Type 2

of good. I was under the impression, like many others, that consuming jaggery is harmless and even healthy, until I found out that while jaggery is good for health because it has certain nutrients, you need to consume it in large quantities to gain any real nourishment from it.[5] Not to mention, jaggery is extremely high in calories and is completely avoidable if you are trying to lose weight. I consume jaggery in very moderate amounts to satisfy the sweet cravings I have every now and then.

If you think about it, once you become a mother, a balanced diet is important. Firstly because you're carrying a baby, secondly because you're nursing and healing and thirdly because now you are a mother for life and your responsibilities have doubled. Naturally, then, it is a good idea to slowly correct all bad eating habits when you get pregnant. If you failed to do so at that time, there's no reason for you to not start now. As they say, better late than never.

I was able to remove foods that were carbohydrate

Diabetes: An Overview of Human Feeding Trials', *Food & Function*, Vol. 10, No. 10, 2019, pp. 6227–43, https://tinyurl.com/yzz6ea83. Accessed on 6 July 2023.
[5]West, Helen, 'What is Jaggery and What Benefits Does it Have?', *Healthline*, 3 July 2023, https://tinyurl.com/2s3wnfzy. Accessed on 6 July 2023.

dense and low on nutrition from my diet. This opened the window to consuming other healthier options, since cutting calories was never the idea at that point. I must reiterate that as a nursing mother, at no point should you want to consciously reduce your calorie intake because that could adversely affect either the nursing or your own health. In fact, the chances of it affecting your own health are much higher because the milk will take the nutrition from your body and feed the child but the mother's body in the process might become weak. So iron, calcium, other minerals, macro and micro nutrients are extremely important for the mother, especially if you start exercising.

There is also no harm in experimenting a little with eliminating certain foods and watching for a couple of days if it gives you any immediate results. I did that with wheat. Once I stopped consuming wheat, I realized that I stopped feeling bloated and felt much lighter. I switched to starchy white rice and that is one of the best forms of carbohydrates.[6] For my roti cravings, I started consuming ragi or amaranth rotis that are a little difficult to cook but completely worth the effort. Eliminating

---

[6]'Starchy Foods and Carbohydrates', NHS, https://tinyurl.com/2a25y5ka. Accessed on 6 July 2023.

wheat is bound to raise many eyebrows; I know it did in my case. Many well-wishers around us feel that it is stupid to eliminate something as essential as wheat from our diet, especially at a time we are nursing. Once again, I would like to point out that when you eliminate something as a trial, you must replace it with another thing, something that is, without a doubt, far better or at least equal in terms of nutrient quotient. Wheat is an excellent grain but could be heavy for a lot of people to digest and this gets worse with age. Besides, it is a good idea to alternate between your choice of daily grains. I now consume wheat rotis every now and then, the only difference being that it is not part of my staple diet anymore. I do not eat it for every meal, every day, like I did earlier. I do eat ragi, jowar, bajra, quinoa and so many other grains, which are also beneficial for me. It helps to know the benefits of other grains that are not so commonly used. Ragi is an extremely good source of protein, carbohydrates, iron, calcium and fibre. It does not contain gluten and its low glycaemic index does not cause an insulin spike, something I was trying to avoid. It is also slower to digest and helps in controlling hunger pangs. All of this goodness with fewer calories. Who

Being Healthy: Post-partum Diet

would say no? The other grains I mentioned are also loaded with benefits. Now, does it sound reasonable to try out this elimination method?

For all mothers who find this too hard to follow, it is all right to eat whatever you desire as long as you are mindful and not overdoing it. This does not include junk food, of course. I would also like to share that as a mother there are times we have to give up the things that we love for our children. Sometimes it is a special blanket that now the child cannot sleep without and the mother finds a way to adjust, or a toy that you choose to buy for the child over a lipstick that you really wanted. Sometimes, you let the child eat the last piece of cake in the fridge, which you had been saving for yourself, right? When I gave up wheat, I knew that this was the start of many things that I would be giving up later, most of them for my children. Only this time, I was doing it for myself.

Moving on, the next thing that I decided was time to let go of, at least for some time, was milk. So yes, the cold coffee finally stopped because I did not want any junk sitting in my body after all. Regarding milk and dairy, there are many different points of view you will come across. Let me begin by telling you my 'milk story'.

I have a double slip disc. The first one happened at the age of 24 and the second one was a few years after I had Areeza. Both slip discs were gradual ones, attributed to incorrect posture while sitting. Between my first slip disc and second, I had completely stopped all forward-bending movements and many other activities of which I became petrified. This caused my back muscles to deteriorate further. I tried a lot of treatments, including an alternate therapy, which was much like regular needle therapy or acupuncture combined with some other kind of science (it was a bit too complicated for me to fathom but I continued my treatment, since it was working like magic). My doctor had advised me to completely let go of milk and wheat, and in fact, had threatened to stop treating me if I did not, saying that his treatment would not have any effect unless I did this. He said that while I could slowly start consuming wheat again on certain occasions, I should never have milk if I wished to avoid aches and pains. Naturally, this piqued my interest. I read further and had frequent arguments with my doctor during my visits. I am positive that deep down, he hated me for all those conversations because I can be like a five-year-old when I do not find something rational. But thanks to

Being Healthy: Post-partum Diet

those conversations and the material I read up about milk consumption, I understood why it can be harmful. Now, there are numerous documentaries available on this topic. In this book, I will give you enough information to pique your curiosity as well, so you can go and bother your own doctors with this, do your own research and form your own opinion.

Here's what my doctor told me: The digestive enzyme for milk, lactase, is no longer present in human bodies after the age of seven, because cow milk was not made for human babies but for calves. Even in people who are not lactose intolerant, the production of lactase decreases with age. I don't know how true this is, but I do know that every time I went crying to Areeza's paediatrician about her not drinking milk, he told me to celebrate. In his words, 'Then dance!' He told me that milk is nothing but an appetite suppressant and nobody should have it unless it is mother's milk. To add to this, I also read that even if our body is capable of digesting cow's milk, it takes us around eight hours to digest one glass of it.[7] Invariably, before it is digested by the stomach

---

[7] 'How Does Milk Digestion Happen?', *Vinmec*, https://tinyurl.com/46vucawu. Accessed on 6 July 2023.

enzymes, we end up having our next meal, thereby putting considerable pressure on our digestive systems. This can potentially damage kidney health, causing all sorts of toxin build-up and other problems while also piling on unhealthy, not to mention unwanted, weight, which we then struggle to lose by cutting down on the other foods that our bodies actually need. This was a lot to process, as I am a huge fan of milk in any form and especially in the form of cold coffee. Yet, I gave up my favourite beverage for more than two years during that time when I saw the wonderful effects myself.

There's a lot of debate around milk consumption and I feel giving it up for at least a month and seeing the effect it has on your body is worth a try before joining either side of the debate. Even now, I do not consume milk on a regular basis but only occasionally, and I have noticed a huge difference in the bloating levels on days that I don't.

Whether you decide to include milk in your post-partum diet or not is a decision you should take in tandem with your doctor, especially while you're breastfeeding. Every time I told somebody of my decision to stop consuming milk, the first question that would pop up is, 'How do you take care of your calcium needs?' Calcium needs are very real during the lactation phase, since our bodies go through a lot during the pregnancy and motherhood journey, so no doctor will risk a nursing mother being deficient in this mineral. Hence, your doctor will ask you to continue taking pregnancy supplements all through your breastfeeding phase and then revisit the need to wean you off when you discontinue breastfeeding. The supplements are meant to take care of your calcium needs for the time being. Besides, calcium in milk is not as well absorbed by the body as the calcium in curd or paneer; if calcium is your reason to consume milk, you may want to switch to curd and paneer instead. I had switched to Greek yogurt for some time.

Apart from eliminating a few things from my diet, there were also certain things that I increased the consumption of to take care of the calorie deficit, primarily, protein. I was not sure if protein supplements that are available in powder form are advisable for breastfeeding mothers, so I simply started having protein-dense foods: eggs, chicken, fish, mutton, more eggs, more chicken, more fish. When I felt hungry out of turn, I knew that my body had been fed too many carbohydrates and too little protein because, if my protein requirement was complete, I would be full for longer. Protein is required to do all kinds of repair work in the body along with repairing the muscles that have broken down during workouts. There's a reason why protein is called the building block of your body.[8] Protein can cause some changes to the way your gut behaves and, hence, an increase in fibre consumption is also an absolute must. I started having broccoli, mushroom and spinach salads every day.

Now that I had taken care of the diet requirement, I needed to slowly stop food consumption at night, a habit I had picked up during night feeds. I took around three months to slowly wean myself off these 'mommy night feeds'. This was not difficult, since Arham slowly reduced his number of night feeds, and as I sleep trained him, he was sleeping for a longer duration. By the time he was six months old, he was completely weaned off night feeds, and since solids had been started, he was able to have a full stomach for longer. Slowly but surely, my night feeds also completely stopped.

---

[8]Bhupathiraju, Shilpa N., and Frank Hu, 'Carbohydrates, Proteins, and Fats', *MSD Manual*, February 2023, https://tinyurl.com/5d5vzj67. Accessed on 6 July 2023.

Being Healthy: Post-partum Diet

The only thing that I now wanted to achieve was keeping my stomach empty for 12 hours for a practice called 'intermittent fasting' or IF. There are different ways IF can be followed, but as a nursing mother, it is extremely important not to starve at any point! It can be detrimental to the mother's health and immediately affect the milk supply, causing your baby to not have a full stomach after each feed. However, 12 hours of going without food, in my opinion, is absolutely necessary when you're neither pregnant nor breastfeeding. The body, the stomach and the digestive system need to rest. I calculated that I slept at around 11.00 p.m. and woke up at 6.00 a.m., which meant seven hours of an empty stomach right there. All I needed to achieve was another three hours. This was not as difficult as it seemed. I started by increasing this time by merely half an hour for the first 15 days. I allowed my body to settle down with this difference, feel comfortable and then increased it by another half an hour for the next 15 days. It took me three months to reach this goal without adversely affecting my health.

In totality, while we take nine months to put on weight during our pregnancies, it is only fair to allow our bodies nine months to get rid of it. I was sure to maintain this pace while also maintaining my sanity. This is the reason I am as fit as I was before I had Arham. For many mothers, these nine months may start at a time that is convenient for them and not necessarily soon after the delivery. Whenever you choose to go down this road, it is important that you allow yourself the time to adjust to every pattern at every step and never expect instant results. The expectation of instant results will only lead to instant failure in achieving your goals because you will see health problems at every stage (besides also risking your milk supply). You may give up in frustration and that will be a completely downhill road to take. Remember, slow and steady wins the race. Even if you take longer than nine months to lose the weight, it is fine. What is important is that you see results at every step and do not let your body stagnate. Also, if you train your body one step at a time, you will realize that it really isn't as hard as we feel! At no point did I shock my body or make it feel like it is not important or that it is not functioning the way I expect it to. I developed a beautiful relationship with my body, and it helped me at every step, too. Today, I feel so proud of my body, not because it looks good but because it allows me to do everything that I ever wanted to.

Being Healthy: Post-partum Diet

For many mothers, not losing the weight gained during pregnancy becomes a challenge and affects them mentally. Mothers have enough mental stress already; this weight-related worry might even affect their mental well-being. Trust me when I say that a little mindfulness gives the body the capability to naturally lose weight, just the way the body naturally puts it on as well. Why, then, do so many mothers become so obsessed with weight loss that their lives start revolving around this issue? In my opinion, body weight only triggers mental stress and this may disturb the perfectly happy life of a new mother. The actual mental disturbance could be because of a variety of factors. Although I feel physically and mentally strong now, it was not the same when I became a mother for the first time.

7

Post-partum Depression and Mental Wellness

It all started when I had Areeza, the breath of fresh air that came into our life, not accidentally but after we had carefully planned her arrival. I vividly remember her being taken out of my body by the doctor and being taken away to be cleaned. She instinctively knew where her mother was and kept staring at me with those huge eyes, not blinking even once. I was so mesmerized looking at those eyes that I forgot to ask the doctor whether it was a girl or a boy! She was taken to a little table nearby while she continued to look at me—my little angel who was going to be my best friend and love me the most in the whole world. Even though I didn't know this at the time, my happiness knew no bounds. From what I read on social media these days, I know that there are many mothers the world over who will relate to this sentiment.

But there was another sentiment I felt soon after Areeza was born, and this I did not get to read much about on social media or hear much about from new mothers. It was a sad, incomplete feeling—a feeling of dejection, of not being good enough, of my life being over as I knew it, a feeling of being trapped, wanting to break free but not wanting to take any action, feeling burdened and fatigued all the time, feeling unhappy and unwanted, feeling like I had too much on my plate and was not getting what I deserved, feeling like I would be consumed by all these feelings, and that nothing of the Chhavi I knew would remain. And although I felt sorry for myself, I felt *guilty* for feeling this way. I felt like I was committing a crime by having such feelings at a time when I should be so happy. How could I feel this way when I had just become a mother? How could I feel this way when every other mother around me felt so proud and satisfied? How could I be unhappy being a mother? How was this my little one's fault if I could not deal with my own responsibilities? It's not like I was the only new mother in the whole world. Surely, all mothers take on their new responsibilities. All these thoughts put so much unnecessary pressure on me that it became extremely suffocating. To top it all, I had this constant urge to do right by my baby. I wanted to give her the best upbringing, always be on my best behaviour around her, always be happy and chirpy in front of my husband because he was the one going out and working so hard the whole day, right? It was only fair. I did not want to be unreasonable and add to anyone's troubles.

No. It was not fair. At the time, I did not know that I was undergoing what is called post-partum depression. It is not very widely spoken about by new mothers because most of them, like me, do not even know that they are suffering from it. The guilt that the feeling generates just adds on to the already existing pressures of being a new mother. Hence, not many take help to deal with this. I understand this now, but I so wish I had spoken to somebody around me at that time. They could have guided me by making me see the situation from a different

Post-partum Depression and Mental Wellness

perspective or by simply making me aware of the existence of this condition. This is the primary reason why I want to talk about post-partum depression in my book.

While my pregnancy and post-partum journey went by smoothly, post-partum depression was also a phase that I went through and it would not be a completely accurate picture if I did not share details about it. Besides, if I also become one of those mothers who only paint a rosy picture of their journey, then I would not be helping the mothers who may struggle a bit like I did. I want this book to genuinely make a difference to every mother's life in a wholesome way.

Dear women, life takes a huge turn once you become a mother. I had carefully timed my pregnancy and it did help that I had prepared myself mentally for a lot of things, like not being able to work for a couple of months, not being able to eat or drink certain foods, not being able to have the lifestyle that I had been living before I conceived, etc. What I was not prepared for were some of the practical changes the baby would bring to my life after its arrival. The first shock was realizing that getting back to work once I had delivered my baby was not going to be as easy as I thought it would be. I had this impression in my head that work (for an actor like me) was difficult during pregnancy solely because the belly shows and it's uncomfortable for the mother to be on the set, and because there aren't many roles which can accommodate a pregnant actor. For this reason, I was prepared for a vacation for the time I was pregnant and started gearing up to get back to work after I delivered. I even got a dream offer when Areeza was only two months old. I was offered the role of the main lead of a TV soap opera; I was to be given a dedicated room for my baby to be comfortable in; I could bring the nanny along; and the generous producers were willing to make the set as comfortable and baby-friendly for my little one as I could have possibly asked for. But even though I had been waiting to get an offer like that, I instinctively found myself saying a vehement no to it because when I actually pictured my baby on a shooting floor, I was horrified! I could not imagine her being raised on a set while I struggled with breastfeeding in between shots. This was the first time I realized that getting back to work was not going to be as easy as I had imagined for a long time because I had completely forgotten to account for the fact that the baby would be entirely dependent

Post-partum Depression and Mental Wellness

on me for basic needs like food. Nor did I realize that I would get so possessive about her! There are many mothers who get back to work early—for some it may be a personal choice and for others it may be a financial necessity—whatever the reason, I know for a fact that a mother needs to be extremely strong emotionally and mentally to be able to take that decision. Let us all take a moment to salute all mothers.

Now let's take a moment to salute mothers like me who chose not to go back to work although work has always been the most integral part of their lives. I know now that this was the starting point of the frustration that nestled deep within me for a long time to come—the frustration that became the trigger for post-partum depression.

I was in for another shock when I realized that all the friends that I had all these years suddenly could not find the time to meet me. It is only later that I realized that it was actually the other way round. I was not able to find the time to meet them because little Areeza always needed me, and when she slept, I too needed to rest. For a bit though, I felt that all my friends were fair-weather friends—just because I could no longer host the rocking parties that I once did, they did not feel the need to have me in their lives anymore. I often found myself snapping at them and getting testy at various points if things didn't go as I visualized them in my head. In retrospect, I feel this whole phase had something positive about it (in a way) because the friends who saw me through that phase and stuck with me were actually the ones who were keepers. The rest of them I could easily filter out from my life, but that became another reason to grieve because that is what post-partum depression does to you—it blocks out all reasons.

My daughter asks me the definition of friends and it really gets me thinking. I still cannot define a friend. Who really is a friend? How do I explain it to her in simple terms? Picture this. My 'best friend' at the time, who I met practically every day throughout my pregnancy, came to visit me one day when I was getting ready to leave for a party to celebrate Mohit's show having completed 1,000 episodes. This was the first time I was stepping out after my delivery and I was very excited about it. I had already set a routine for little Areeza and knew that she would sleep by 7.00 p.m., after which she would need a dream feed at 10.30 p.m., which I had freshly expressed and handed over to the nanny, and then she would subsequently wake up at 3.00 p.m. for another night feed and I would be there for that. Now the only thing that needed to be planned was the dress I would be wearing for this party, as there were still many clothes in my wardrobe that did not complement my new body as a nursing mother. It was not anything to worry about since my 'best friend' was there to help me out. To my sheer horror, she told me how fat I looked in the dress that I had selected, and how my cellulite was showing, and then tried to lamely cover up saying it was okay since men liked fat women! She body shamed me, objectified me and belittled me. I instantly knew that she would be the first 'friend' I would eliminate from my social circle for the rest of my life.

I did not say anything at the time, and even though she realized her mistake later and apologized, I can never forget the look of victory and sadistic pleasure I saw in her eyes that night. So yes, some of these 'friends' can really make a new mother feel out of sorts. I went to the party and was complimented by almost everyone on how lovely I looked and I was even asked about how I had lost the weight so fast. But the damage had been done—the remark that came from somebody who had seen me through every struggle made a deeper impact than the polite ones from strangers. This was when another provocateur for post-partum depression started to show up. The body weight I had gained, even though miniscule, really started to play havoc with my mind.

Another reason I felt low most of the time was a severe and sudden lack of any time that I could refer to as 'me-time'. I had been used to spending all 24 hours in a day doing literally everything that I wanted to do, and now suddenly everything was happening as per the baby's schedule. No more late-night TV, no more relaxing strolls in the mall, no more idle strolls in the park, no more yoga, no more going to coffee shops, no more of anything at all that I wanted to do! So, when Mohit would come home from work, I thought I could vent about my day to him, but I would wind up feeling too tired and sleepy and guilt-stricken to tell him anything about my own day when he himself looked so exhausted. It just felt unfair to bombard him with my problems at that time. I bet most of you have felt that way at some point or the other. I guess women have been conditioned to act in such a way since the time we are born—to be sensitive towards others, to not prioritize what we want

Post-partum Depression and Mental Wellness

but listen to others. Or maybe it is the hormones that make us the way we are. Nevertheless, keeping all of it inside me did far more harm. Obviously venting to a 'friend' was out of the question since I didn't know who my true friends were. I also felt wary of being judged and labelled a 'bad mother'.

Around this time, I went through another life-altering episode. On my birthday, I was out with a few friends for lunch and was cheerfully discussing my motherhood problems. I happened to tell them how badly I needed a break and if I could leave Areeza with Mohit and the nanny for just two days, I would go to my favourite holiday destination, Goa, which would do wonders for me. Suddenly, the vibe in the room changed from a friendly one to a judgemental one, and before I knew it, the conversation started to go south. Everybody began to throw judgemental remarks at me and not one of them understood the sensitive state of mind I was in.

Dear mothers, when I look back, I wish I had had the courage to defy everybody and take the much-needed time off. I would have been a much happier mother. So, a word of advice, if you ever feel like taking a break, *please do*! You are entitled to it and no number of judgemental remarks should make you stop. Judgements are a part and parcel of life, although I know they sting far more when you're judged as a mother rather than just an individual. Remember, you neither need approval from anybody nor do you need to explain yourself to anybody. If you ever feel like taking some time off, like I did, all you need to do is to take your husband or your immediate support system into confidence and decide the travel dates in tandem with their availability. I followed this thumb rule when I had Arham and I was able to enjoy my motherhood journey with him far more than I did when Areeza was a baby. The fear of being labelled a bad mother is panic-inducing for every woman. Just nip it in the bud and tell yourself that you are the best mother because, trust me, it is true in all likelihood.

To add to every new mother's misery, the responsibilities that you are suddenly loaded with are too overwhelming. I was 31 when Areeza was born. I was independent, mature, wiser than many. There are so many young mothers who are in their mid-twenties when they have babies. It is such a tender age to bear the responsibility of a new life, isn't it? I now realize that if I can feel burdened at such a mature age, a 20-something new mother would really

Post-partum Depression and Mental Wellness

have her hands full. I was six days post-partum when I got up from the bed to resume all duties as a mother, including bathing, massaging, putting the baby to bed, changing the diaper, etc. There are many mothers who do this from day one, along with their domestic chores, like cooking and cleaning. Mental health can truly be a struggle for such mothers. On top of all these changes that happen in a new mother's life, a very significant one is the hormones playing havoc. It is not that mothers are not capable of handling any of these pressures, it is just that new mothers are way too emotional and sensitive. Their health is not at its best since the recovery and healing from childbirth takes time. But no matter how long this healing takes, a new mother is required to take on her responsibilities the minute her baby is born. The breastfeeding journey is also not something that can be estimated prior to it being experienced.

Take me, for example. My breastfeeding let-down took a good two days and Areeza, like most babies, was also struggling to find the correct position to latch on. How quickly the let-down happens depends on how quickly the baby learns how to suckle because it is the suckling response that leads to the let-down and in all probability things take roughly around two days to settle. I knew all this from my Lamaze classes and yet cried a lot thinking there must be something wrong with me. Areeza was given a top feed at the hospital. There are no words to describe how guilty that made me feel. In that moment, I felt like I would not be able to breastfeed her because now she will learn how to get fed without sucking and that was crucial for my own let-down. I am very happy to say that like most mothers, these were just my fears and I went on to exclusively breastfeed her till the time she switched to solids.

All these factors, combined with no help to deal with those, makes for the perfect recipe for post-partum depression. While it does sound extremely daunting, not everyone goes through this. The mothers who do go through it, they should assured that this too shall pass. That is the first piece of good news. The second is that by merely knowing about it, you can understand yourself better and be better equipped to deal with it. But the best news of all is that by taking a little help, post-partum depression can be potentially avoided or dealt with in a better manner. Let me tell you the mistakes I made that I now understand. I used my understanding to combat

Post-partum Depression and Mental Wellness

any such feelings after having my second baby.

First and foremost, take help. Whatever help you can get—help with the baby, help with the cooking, help with other responsibilities, help with daily chores, like deciding what is to be cooked, doing the laundry, doing the dishes, cleaning up the room, sending the clothes for ironing, getting the door when the bell rings, etc. When Arham was born, I made sure to completely stop going into the kitchen unless it was for my own work. And when I did, I controlled the urge to start cleaning up because even if I wanted to do it at the time, I would get exhausted. I would also not have the energy to attend to baby duties, which I did not want to neglect no matter how much help I had at hand. When I had had Areeza, I was the one mostly attending to her during the days as well as the nights because I felt that there was no reason to wake up another person, mostly my husband, to burp her or change her and disrupt his sleep as well. This had added to my sleep deprivation and the mental imbalance that I was already dealing with. So, the second time, when Mohit offered to attend to Arham during the nights, I happily accepted and went back to sleep. There were times when we both stayed up together and it felt so much better to spend sleepless nights together rather than all alone with a crying baby. In fact, it gives rise to the feeling of love and togetherness and adds to the fact that both of you are raising a baby together. Those were the sleepless nights that I particularly enjoyed. To be honest, Arham has such a special bond with his father and I know in my heart that it is because he has slept more in his Abu's (as he calls him) arms than his Mummy's. Looking at Mohit putting him to sleep after a night feed would make me feel so secure that even amidst his cries, I would sleep soundly knowing that he is well taken care of. This was never the case with Areeza because I felt guilty asking for help, as if it was my responsibility alone to look after her at night. I feel we have also been conditioned to think that one person in the house is the breadwinner while the other is responsible for raising the kids. Since I was not ready to go back to work yet, the person shouldering all the domestic burden would have had to be me. I am so glad that this notion is changing with equal parenting catching up fast with the new generation of parents. Not only is it more fun, it is also healthier than just blindly playing the role of a perfect mother that you assign to yourself, or is forced upon you by society.

Post-partum Depression and Mental Wellness

The other thing that I consciously tried doing the second time was taking a break from everything around me at various times during the day. Whether you want to call it me-time or rejuvenation is up to you, but these little moments that I spent by myself made a huge difference on how I felt emotionally. It also made a positive impact on how I handled the little one as well as my older one, who by now had her own set of unique problems that needed attention. One of the things that can add a lot of stress to a second-time mother is the way the older child deals with the new one's arrival. I would like to advise second-time mothers to be extremely patient with the older child; although the little one at this point looks as though they need you much more than the older one, I cannot stress enough that it is in fact the other way round. While the little one has no idea what is happening if you leave them crying for a minute or two, the older child will be deeply impacted by being left alone by the mother—it can leave a long-lasting impression on them.

Areeza started feeling left out when my breastfeeding journey with Arham began. She would want attention exactly when it was time to feed Arham. She would throw a fit saying she wanted me when I would take Arham on my lap and no amount of explaining helped at that point. Had I taken Arham and let her cry at these times, deep-rooted feelings of jealousy would have crept into an otherwise affectionate sibling. A few times, I left Arham to cry and patiently attended to what Areeza needed me for; this made her feel uncomfortable and she herself told me to hold him because he was so tiny and he wanted Mama.

I would also include Areeza in my breastfeeding time with Arham. In fact, we enjoyed our moments together— Arham would be happily (and quietly) suckling while Areeza would sit next to me and tell me all the stories in the world that she wanted to. It would be bonding time for the three of us. Sometimes, she would sing songs for Arham, would tickle his feet when he would doze off on my breast, would run to get me a wet wipe or a diaper— slowly but surely these moments became crucial in the bonding that I now see between the two of them. I always remembered that Areeza was big enough to understand her emotions and I, as a mother, am responsible for her happiness since it is not an easy task to share the one person you love the most in the world, your own mother who is irreplaceable, with another person who you still must learn to love. The choice to decide between which

Post-partum Depression and Mental Wellness

child to attend to for a second-time mother is not an easy one. It can cause a lot of misery and guilt when you don't know whether you chose the right kid at the time. Even when you have made a choice, you always get the feeling of having made the wrong one. So, for all second-time mothers, stay calm, and soon you will find your own way of attending to both together, just the way I did.

Coming back to me-time, I took a break from everything whenever I started to feel even slightly overwhelmed. I would either sit on my swing for a while or simply lock myself up in the bathroom if there was nowhere else to go. I would hand over Arham to anybody who was available at the time, or just request them to watch him for five minutes, and five minutes were all I needed to centre myself. When I was on the swing, I would simply stare at nature. Not having mobiles or gadgets around was a strict rule that I followed. I feel that gadgets have strongly increased the stress our brains undergo—it could be stemming from the physical strain or the comparisons we draw while scrolling through social media. On the other hand, looking at nature, trees swaying with the breeze, birds chirping and flying in the sky, flowers falling from trees with the breeze, simply helped me feel grounded.

It made me realize, and it still does, how simple life is and how we complicate it. I felt more attuned to the fact that all we need is love, food on the table and a roof over our heads. It makes me realize the importance of what I have and all that I have been blessed with.

The moment I start thinking of my blessings, the first two things that come to my mind are the two adorable kids I have, even though they cry and crib and throw tantrums. Isn't it the same with everyone? Even during my worst phases, I would just feel like going and picking up Arham and consoling him. What is also important to realize though, dear mothers, is that it is okay for the baby to cry at times. I know how it feels when the baby cries uncontrollably and as a mother it drives us crazy to not know what to do to soothe our own baby, and this can truly be overwhelming. I have cried at times with Areeza when I couldn't soothe her. With Arham, I was prepared for this and by just telling myself that 'it is okay for him to cry at times', I felt better. I took these five-minute breaks whenever I could not handle it anymore and, let me tell you, every time I came back from my break, I instinctively knew how to calm him down because I myself felt calm and centred, and the baby always catches on to that vibe.

But all said and done, I would still feel hurt, sad and unhappy, and that would make me more guilty than ever—how can somebody complain when they have so much that it can be the subject of another's envy? Does that feel familiar? This is hormones playing havoc on a new mother's mind. It is not that I always felt like this. Some days were worse and some days I felt like my usual chirpy, positive self. On days I felt low, I snapped for no reason, I felt like crying at times or even felt like writing depressing verses. Then all of a sudden, it would pass, and I would feel really upbeat. I so wish I had spoken to somebody about it or at least had an inkling that these were classic signs of depression or, in my case, post-partum.

Before I could even realize what was wrong with me, these symptoms started fading away on their own. Areeza might have been a year old or even a bit more when I found myself thinking of ways to revive my work and of creating new avenues for myself. I had long realized that getting back to the life of a TV actor was not going to much of an option for me anymore, since I was never going to be a mother who could entrust someone else to raise her kid. Thankfully, I had that choice to make and made the choice of staying home with Areeza for as long as I could and then subsequently started a business of my own, on my own terms. However, from feeling like the world had ended to coming out stronger was a tough struggle. Fortunately, there are many avenues for help today for mothers struggling with post-partum depression. Simply talking to a near one can help you feel better. If that doesn't help, there are professionals too that offer help to mothers. These professionals are fully equipped in dealing with such matters.

All I want to say to every mother and every woman who is reading this is that having a baby for the first time is a herculean task for anyone and in no way should you undermine your own capabilities. But just because you are a mother or are going to be one does not mean that you possess superhuman abilities and are not allowed to have a temper or a tantrum of your own. In fact, in my opinion, a mother should be allowed to have a temper far more than anyone else because I know how much patience and hard work it takes to raise a baby. I know how many times a mother has to put her own needs aside to attend to the baby's needs, and how many times she puts her own desires on hold to fulfil those of her children.

Post-partum Depression and Mental Wellness

I know how many times I have given up on basic needs, like going to the toilet when the baby cries or left my coffee only to throw it out later, because that's the kind of busy a mother gets. And for every little sacrifice, the least she should be allowed to do is throw a little tantrum every now and then.

I have long stopped feeling the need to please others or do things according to people around me. I have learnt the hard way that people will not appreciate what you do for them or what you sacrifice for them if you do not spell it out, and spelling it out will wipe away all your efforts put into it in the first place. So, I choose to do the things that make me happy. Sometimes, it may not be cooking a meal for a visiting guest to make them feel special, but cleaning and sorting out the kids' wardrobe or study desk instead. I have learnt the importance of putting myself first. Of course, this does not mean that one should be selfish; it simply means that if you are happy, you will be able to make everyone around you happy and relaxed. And as the adage goes, 'Love thy neighbour as thyself.' We usually remember to love our neighbour, but often forget to love ourselves. And how are we supposed to love our neighbour if we don't know how to love ourselves? So, yes, prioritizing myself is something I have trained myself to do over the years, and I have received the strength to do that after I became a mother.

Once you become a mother, you will always be a mother. You will behave like a mother, think like a mother, act like a mother. Even after you get out of the tough early phase, which you will definitely learn to master, you might continue to feel the daily pressures of being a mother. Before you get complacent with not giving yourself priority, I would like to share with you a few simple tips on how you can take out time for what you love while also being a hands-on mother like I am.

8

The Art of Time Management

Arham was born in May 2019, and the deadly Covid-19 pandemic hit the world in November 2019. Soon after, March 2020 saw the nationwide lockdown being imposed. Everything came to a standstill. Offices and shops shut, roads were empty, the concept of working from home was introduced. Drastically, for some working mothers, domestic workers were not allowed to enter buildings in lieu of the newly introduced social distancing norms. Many people suffered huge losses. However, many found new livelihoods, honed other skills, started home businesses, while others lost all hope. I had my own share of problems.

By then, I was fully into the content creation business. We shot content, which needed us to get to a shoot location, hire a crew, give the footage to an editor for post-production, for which we had three units in our own office, and then the social media implementation followed, based on the marketing strategy for each piece of content. At that point, we had a minimum of two videos being created and posted every week. With the lockdown, the shooting stopped. Then, two of my editors quit, leaving me with just one who was working from home. Unable to deliver film footage physically, we had to upload it online, which took a day, the editor downloading it took another day and finally there was the online process of editing, which was also really slow and depended on the network of both parties. Then, my personal assistant who helped me with all my social media work quit because he could not manage working from home. The chief assistant of the company left, too. Suddenly, I was left to do a lot of this work on my own.

At that time, Arham was only 10 months old. He had started crawling and needed constant attention. Areeza had started online classes for which she, too, needed me

The Art of Time Management

to sit with her. Being a Waldorf child[9], she had never even touched a mobile phone, let alone any other gadget. To add to this, we also had to take over the tasks of mopping, cleaning and cooking, as our help had left. How was I supposed to manage any of it if I did not know how to manage my time? I was repeatedly asked in interviews how I was managing the workload and the domestic responsibilities. I never had a negative thing to say because the way I looked at it, I learnt so much during that phase that, if anything, I was thanking the universe for the opportunities that were brought to me.

I am now prepared for any situation and am completely self-sufficient. I learnt how to edit. I single-handedly took charge of all our social media platforms. I launched a few new shows that I shot from home and they became extremely popular during the lockdown. Mohit and I alternated cooking and cleaning; we even worked out every day for an hour at home, which became our cherished family time together. We also got all our shoot equipment home

---

[9]Waldorf education, developed by Rudolf Steiner, is a holistic teaching approach focussing on the students' imagination and creativity. Steiner believed that every child should be given 'individualized' attention. The use of gadgets is prohibited in the first seven years of life in order to limit exposure and enhance imagination.

and Mohit took charge of the camera and lighting while I took charge of acting and taking care of the children. We found perfect harmony in the way we did things. The reason I am sharing this is not because I want to be pompous. I'm sharing this because I feel it is necessary to hear for every mother, especially working mothers who went through this particular phase, handling a plethora of responsibilities side by side, constantly putting their own needs on the back burner.

So, here is a step-by-step guide on how I manage my time with the kids, the domestic chores and the office work. These are suggestions that you can apply in your life too and, hopefully, it will help you just as it has helped me.

First, set a sleep routine for the baby. The sooner you do this, the easier it gets. I started setting a sleep routine for Areeza when she was all of two months old and managed to complete my mission by the time she was four months old. With Arham, I started at day one, and succeeded by the time he was only one month old. Thanks to the rhythm I followed with him, he was sleeping through the night by the time he was only three months old. There are various methods to do this. I read multiple books on this topic, but the ones that helped

The Art of Time Management

me the most were *Secrets of the Baby Whisperer* by Tracy Hogg and Melinda Blau and *12 Hours' Sleep by 12 Weeks Old* by Suzy Giordano and Lisa Abidin. Needless to say, I tweaked certain ideas suggested in the books to fit my own baby's needs.

The basic principle every book follows is that you set a routine following the baby's natural sleep and feed cycle and then make sure you stick to it no matter what your plans for the day are. I shifted all my plans as per the kids' routine. I still do. This is important because if the child is well fed and has slept well, the chances of them crying are low, and even if they do cry, one look at the clock and, as per their routine, you instantly know what they need—whether it is to sleep or to eat.

Once the baby's routine is set, you will know what your windows of free time are. These are the different time slots when the baby naps. Once I knew this about Arham, I started carefully planning out my day around these windows.

First, Arham and Areeza would have their early morning meal. They would then get busy playing, and it doubled as their workout time. This would be followed by a nap for Arham, a window during which I would either cook breakfast or clean, depending on whether it was my turn that day. Then, I would massage Arham and bathe him. I would feed breakfast to both the kids, after which Arham would fall asleep again while Areeza would attend her online classes. This used to be the window to cook lunch, which never took more than an hour and 15 minutes. If Mohit would cook, I would do the dishes and vice versa. We would be done with all this by 12.30 p.m. and would then take a break to bathe, freshen up, etc. After lunch, when Arham would take another nap while Areeza just played around, I would sit down to do my office work. I would give them a quick snack around 5.00 p.m. and then resume work. Work would go on till 6.00 p.m. and then it would be time for Arham's bedtime routine. He would mostly fall asleep by 7.00 p.m., post dinner, which was mostly khichdi for him at that time. Then, we would cook our dinner. Around 8.00 p.m., we would all eat, following which Areeza would be put to bed by 9.00 p.m. We would not work post 9.00 p.m. and instead enjoy some couple time and crash for the day by 10.00 or 11.00 p.m. There were days that looked a bit different, depending on whether we had extra work, but there was nothing that was not manageable.

The Art of Time Management

This was a workable model, and it still is, because we, as mothers, can understand the needs of our children. However, if you try to tell the child that they should understand your needs and not disturb you at the moment, chances are that they will throw a fit and you will end up wasting more time placating them than you would have if you just heard them out the first time they disturbed you. This is yet another thing I have learnt from experience. So, the best thing to do is to find the time to do your own work when you know there will be no child to disturb you. This helped me complete my tasks faster and more efficiently.

One more thing to do is to start creating a to-do list. Short and doable. I personally feel really stressed when there are a lot of things on my mind and I feel that the burden will make me forget something and that will be disastrous. But merely jotting it down, I feel like half my job is done because it does not look half as daunting on paper as it does on your mind. What is also important is to not try to multitask. Contrary to the popular notion that multitasking gets more work done faster, I believe that it only takes away the focus from the job at hand. So, I try to do one thing at a time, finish it, and then move on to the next one. That way, I can keep striking out things from my to-do list and that always gives me a unique sense of satisfaction.

The other thing I would like to point out is that it is all right to not be able to complete a scheduled task. The world will not come crashing down. In fact, if you fail to accomplish something on a Friday, give yourself the weekend off and get to it again on Monday. You should not beat yourself about it. What is important is that you set definite goals for yourself. Random objectives like planning to do something but not deciding the actual steps that you need to take to accomplish that objective are totally futile and only add a lot more pressure on the mind, thereby making you less efficient. A good example of this would be wanting to start a home business, having an idea, but not knowing the first step to take to start moving in that direction. Even if you can chalk out a plan on paper and set a time limit for yourself to achieve it, that right there is a lot of work done.

But above all, dear mothers, let me tell you this, once you let yourself relax, take one step at a time, learn to adapt, be a little flexible with yourself and, most importantly, learn to be kind to yourself. There is literally nothing you cannot achieve. In my opinion, just the way you should make a to-do list for the things you want to accomplish but do not have the time for, you should also make a list of things that you constantly tell yourself you cannot do. I have heard many mothers make statements like, '*Ye toh main kar hi nahi sakti* (This is impossible for me)', '*Kehna asaan hai karna mushkil* (It is easier said than done)', or '*Aap ke liye easy hai, mere jaison ke liye nahi* (It is easy for you, not for people like me)' and '*Mere paas toh time he nahi hai* (I simply do not have the time)'.

I believe you will be able to achieve whatever you have set your mind to. Just like if you have an obsession for red cars, you will spot many red cars on the road, and if you keep thinking about food, you will keep feeling hungry, if you keep thinking about your failures, you will only face failures. Instead, if you choose to focus on your dreams and objectives, you will find ways to make them happen. The body achieves what the mind believes. The point that I am trying to make is whether your goal is to have your dream body or to be financially independent, if you believe you can, you can.

For me, the endeavour to be physically fit is where all discipline starts. The days I can begin by prioritizing my fitness are the ones I am able to take full control of.

Before you put this book down, let me remind you to realize what an amazing journey you have embarked upon, right from the initial stages of pregnancy through the post-partum period. Remember the physical, emotional, and mental changes you have experienced and commend yourself for your resilience. Do not forget the importance of self-care during both pregnancy and the post-partum phase. Prioritize your own well-being by nurturing your physical, emotional and mental health. Remember, you deserve care and attention as you navigate the joys and challenges of parenthood.

I would also like to reiterate the importance of a nutritious diet for both mother and baby. Be mindful of consuming what your body needs and what your heart desires, but always strike the right balance and refrain from overdoing anything that is harmful for you. Remember the essential nutrients needed during pregnancy and post-partum, and the benefits of a well-rounded, balanced meal plan. If needed, do not shy away from consulting with healthcare professionals or nutritionists for personalized guidance.

Once again, the benefits of regular physical activity

during and after pregnancy cannot be emphasized enough. Maintain strength, flexibility and good cardiovascular health. No matter how you look and feel about your body, do not forget to acknowledge and appreciate what it has given you. Start gradually and consult with healthcare providers for individualized recommendations.

And, finally, dear mothers, never forget that our bodies go through hormonal transformations every month even when we are not pregnant. Pregnancy only makes it so much more fragile. We are the first ones to understand our own needs; it is up to us whether we prioritize our mental health or physical fitness.

Before you continue on this beautiful journey, ask yourself: What is the thing that defines you? Not as a mother, not as a wife, but as you. Then, go find yourself.

Before I conclude, I would like to highlight the fact that this is just the beginning. Once you start, there will be no stopping you. In fact, you will be able to continue to grow and flourish as a woman and as a mother. I thank you for picking up my book and being a part of my journey and experiencing it as your own. I hope I could make a difference in your life in a positive way. Love and peace from me to you.

Acknowledgements

I want to thank my husband, Mohit Hussein, who stood by me every step of the way while I wrote this book, sometimes taking charge of my other responsibilities and sometimes reminding me to take a break. This would not be possible without you.

I also want to thank my daughter, Areeza Hussein for being the most understanding little girl to allow me the luxury to always be creative and enterprising. Thank you, my little girl! You will always be my best friend.

www.ingramcontent.com/pod-product-compliance
Lightning Source LLC
Chambersburg PA
CBHW020852160426
43192CB00007B/890